ASCENT

ASCENT

THE GAP BETWEEN
POTENTIAL AND PROGRESS
IS THE ROOM YOU'RE IN

Scott Joseph

Dedication

To my father,
who showed me what standards look like long before I understood why they matter. And to the leaders who refused to let me stay the same when it would have been easier to.

Contents

Foreword 3

Preface 5

Prologue 7

1 | The Room That Changed Everything 9

Interlude: The First Spark 21

2 | The Moment Relationships Became the Strategy 27

3 | The Reality Behind Masterminds 47

4 | Why Environments Outperform Effort 57

5 | The Anatomy of a Better Room 67

6 | How Better Rooms Expand What You're Able to
Think Through 77

7 | What Better Rooms Do to Your Identity 85

8 | The Mechanics of High-Performance Rooms 97

9 | What High-Standard Rooms Require From You 113

10 | When You're Ready for the Room That Changes Everything . . 119

Conclusion 133

A Gift for You 135

Epilogue 139

About The Author 143

Thank You 145

Foreword

Scott has a unique ability to crystallize environments ("rooms") that realize a combination of awareness and process that evokes the powerful potential that one knows they have and/or is looking for, that they can't seem to achieve or make time to realize actually happens. This book provides a tactical and powerfully simple formula for triangulating: fundamental awareness, focusing decisions, and selecting and/or curating environments to move through, with regard to time in a way that is undeniably achievable regardless of how "busy" one might believe they are.

- John Garcia | Managing Partner, Solyco Capital

Preface

I didn't set out to write a book about rooms, environments or leadership dynamics. I wrote this because, over time, I started noticing something that didn't line up with the way success is usually explained and I wanted to address it.

I've been building businesses since 1991. I've been inside enough conversations, partnerships, and decision cycles to recognize when effort and intelligence are the limiting factors, and when they're not. What stood out wasn't how often leaders lacked answers. It was how often capable people were operating below their potential, without realizing why.

For a long time, I assumed this was simply the cost of experience, increased responsibility, added complexity, and a greater sense of caution. That explanation worked until I started paying attention to how differently the same leaders showed up in different settings. Their thinking changed. Their posture changed. The way decisions took shape changed. Not because they were trying harder, but because the environment required something different from them.

That observation stayed with me.

I wrote this book to examine that difference for you. Not as a theory, and not as a critique, but as a practical reality with no name in which most leaders live. The rooms you spend time in shape what feels normal. They influence how much precision you bring, how much challenge you tolerate, and how often unfinished ideas get carried forward instead of resolved.

I didn't write this book to argue that one kind of room is better than another. I wrote it to make the mechanics visible. Once you see how standards form and how behavior adapts to them, it becomes much harder to ignore the role the environment plays in your own growth.

What follows isn't advice and it isn't a system to implement. It's a way of looking more clearly at the spaces where decisions are shaped, relationships are formed, and momentum is either reinforced or quietly eroded. The goal isn't to tell you what to change, but to help you recognize what's already changing you.

That clarity is what this book will provide.

Prologue

Most leaders don't realize when a room stops helping them.

It doesn't happen abruptly, and it doesn't announce itself. It usually shows up during a conversation that should have mattered. You chose to be there. The people around the table are capable, experienced, and worth listening to. The discussion is respectful, thoughtful, and familiar enough to feel productive.

At some point, you notice that you're contributing in ways that are expected of you. You know which ideas will land. You know how to frame your perspective so it fits the tone of the room. You leave nothing exposed, nothing half-formed, nothing that requires anyone else to press you for clarity.

The meeting ends and nothing feels wrong. You're respected. You were useful. You didn't waste your time. And yet, when you step away, there's a quiet recognition that something important didn't happen. Not because the conversation was bad, but because it never asked anything more of you than what you already knew how to give.

That moment is easy to overlook. Comfort makes things familiar. Experience makes it reasonable. You tell yourself that value accumulates over time, that not every conversation needs to stretch you, and that consistency matters more than disruption. All of that sounds right, which is why the pattern can repeat without drawing attention to itself.

What changes, slowly, is how you show up. You stop bringing questions that don't yet have shape. You stop testing ideas that might need friction to improve. You stay inside the version of yourself that already fits the room, because there's no incentive to step beyond it.

We'll begin at that point of recognition.

Not when ambition fades and not when results collapse, but when capable leaders realize that the environments they trust most are no longer asking for their best thinking. This book is about understanding how that happens, what it costs over time, and how rooms quietly shape the kind of leader you become without ever asking your permission.

The Room That Changed Everything

OI

For most of my entrepreneurial life, I operated as if needing help was a weakness. I never said it out loud (most entrepreneurs don't), but I lived like it was true. I was introverted. I didn't enjoy networking. I believed that if I worked hard enough and stayed focused, I could solve every problem with effort, discipline and grinding, and because I had early success, that belief grew roots.

At the time, my entire identity as an entrepreneur was tied to the company I founded — J&L Marketing, a direct and digital marketing agency serving automotive dealerships across the country. What started as a small idea quickly turned into a national operation. I built the company from the ground up, surrounded myself with a strong sales team that could open doors anywhere in the country, and relied on an operations group who cared deeply about delivering exceptional work and would run through walls for our clients. Money was coming in. Opportunities were growing. On the surface, everything pointed to the conclusion that I had cracked the code.

Looking back now, I realize the real blind spot wasn't in the business... it was in me. Early success had convinced me that the habits that built the company were the same habits required to scale it. They weren't. Because I couldn't see it at the time, I kept operating with the same mindset long after the business needed a different version of me.

It wasn't the work or the people that limited us in those early years. It was the environment I kept myself in.

A Start That Should Have Been Even Stronger

The first couple of decades at J&L were filled with wins. We built a reputation in the automotive industry that most companies would envy. Clients trusted us. Our name carried weight, yet all of that happened inside of a closed loop.

My entire world was the auto industry. The only external conversations I ever had were at trade shows, where people recycled the same ideas and congratulated each other on doing things the same way again and again. Those rooms didn't push me. They reinforced the limits I didn't even realize I had placed on myself.

Our team was strong. Our model worked. But because I didn't intentionally expose myself to people who thought bigger, faster, and more creatively than I did, I stopped challenging myself. That is the part I would change if I could go back. We could have grown farther, faster, and with far less friction if I had known how much perspective I was missing.

The problem wasn't the business. The problem was the rooms.

The Breaking Point

Even with all of the success, the strain eventually caught up. We didn't have documented processes or cross-training. Workloads weren't balanced. Too much knowledge lived in people's heads, which meant the same handful of employees were carrying an impossible weight.

Even worse, because I believed it was all on my shoulders, I became the biggest bottleneck in the company.

One night brought it all into focus. I was sitting in front of my computer, exhausted, answering what felt like an endless stream of emails, every one of them asking me to solve something. A serious issue came through from operations: we had five marketing campaigns scheduled over the next week that still needed on-site representatives, and we were out of people. No backup. No redundancy. No room for error. Everyone was waiting on me to decide what to do.

That was the pattern. Everything flowed to my inbox. Every decision needed my approval. Every fire was mine to put out.

I wasn't frustrated anymore... I was numb. After two straight years of grinding harder while sales plateaued, something in me started to feel defeated. That feeling forced me to confront what I'd been avoiding.

It wasn't the workload that made me pause. It was the realization that, unless something changed, I could lose everything I had built. Comfort is a strange thing. You think you want to break out of it, but subconsciously you don't. Growth feels risky. Going backward feels terrifying. My ego was driving the bus back then. I worried about what failing publicly would look like, especially to the people who had doubted me when I first started.

That night, I finally confronted the truth head-on: I had taken the company as far as I could on my own. **Something had to change.**

The part I didn't want to say out loud was this: I wasn't sure I deserved the success I already had.

I turned to my wife, and said, "I don't care what it costs. I need help. I can't keep doing this."

That was the moment the gap between who I was and who I needed to become came into view.

The Room That Opened My Eyes

Shortly after that night, I made a decision that changed the trajectory of my career. I registered for Tony Robbins' Business Mastery event in Chicago. I didn't go for motivation. I went because I had hit a wall I didn't know how to climb, and I needed to be around people who were further along than I was.

Chicago was the first time I was surrounded by entrepreneurs who had already solved the problems I was drowning in. They weren't interested in my highlight reel. They didn't care what I had already accomplished. Their only focus was what I was trying to build next...and why I wasn't thinking bigger.

Being in that room forced me to confront the limitations I had been carrying for years. During breakout sessions I opened up about the chaos inside the business; process gaps, bottlenecks, inefficiencies, and the lack of clarity that was holding everyone back. Instead of nodding politely, people dug in. They asked real questions. They challenged assumptions. They shared how they had navigated similar issues, and they helped me map out a plan that made more sense than anything I had come up with on my own.

When I got home, I acted immediately. I hired our first VP of Operations, José Zabaneh, and he made a massive impact from day one. He documented every process, established clarity and structure, introduced Kaizen (a business philosophy that focuses on continuous improvement), and built the foundation for scalable growth. Within a year, the entire company felt lighter, more efficient, and more aligned.

Chicago didn't just give me strategies. It showed me what happens when you get in the right room.

Success That Hid the Next Ceiling

The clarity I gained in Chicago didn't just reshape how I operated in the moment, it became the first of several shifts that would reshape my leadership over the years. J&L grew quickly after that period. The operational structure we built, the discipline José brought to the organization, and the way the company began running with more stability created the foundation for expansion long before I realized how significant it would be.

As the business strengthened, new opportunities emerged. That next wave of growth is what put me in the position to acquire Johnson City Honda in 2004, Cape Girardeau Honda in 2006, and West County Honda in 2011. Each store thrived under the leadership of managing partners I respected deeply. That success reinforced a truth I wish I had learned earlier: *you don't scale by doing more... you scale by trusting the right people.*

But the growth cycle didn't last forever. After the dealership acquisitions, J&L hit a different kind of plateau, not the volatility that existed before Chicago, but a slower, quieter ceiling that happens when a business matures and the leader hasn't yet made the next internal shift. That's when I started seeking new rooms again, not because the company was failing, but because I could feel myself outgrowing the way I was thinking.

The Cost That Didn't Look Like Failure

The part I didn't see at first was the associated cost. Not the obvious kind that shows up when revenue drops or clients leave, but the kind that accumulates while a business keeps producing and everyone assumes that means things are fine.

After the dealership acquisitions, J&L didn't look unhealthy. We were still closing deals. Long-term clients stayed with us. The sales team continued to perform. From the outside, it read as stability. Inside the business, though, standing still was getting more expensive every quarter.

Costs never pause just because revenue holds. Wages rose as the cost of living increased. Vendor contracts reset higher than before. We added people to keep up with demand, then added management layers to coordinate the people we had added. Software tools multiplied to compensate for gaps that processes should have handled. Compliance became heavier as the business matured. None of this felt dramatic in isolation, but together it created a constant squeeze on margin. The top line didn't flash red, but the bottom line felt tighter every year.

What made this phase dangerous was that nothing felt careless or undisciplined. Every decision made sense in the moment. When something slowed down, the instinct wasn't to stop and rethink the structure. It was to push harder, add capacity, and rely on experience to bridge the gaps. That approach had worked before, so it didn't register as a warning when it stopped working as well.

The real cost only became obvious in hindsight. Decisions took longer because more people needed to weigh in. Simple changes required alignment across teams that had grown dependent on each other instead of clearly accountable. Ownership blurred as responsibility spread horizontally rather than being forced into defined lanes. Instead of fixing inefficiencies at the root, the organization learned how to work around them. Not because anyone was lazy or unaware, but because correcting them would have meant admitting that the model itself needed to evolve again. That's a hard thing to face when the business still looks healthy on paper.

Personally, this was the most subtle ceiling I had hit as a leader. I didn't feel stuck. I felt like I was doing what the business needed from me. The company was profitable. People depended on it. We had built something meaningful, and my instinct was to protect it by staying close and staying involved. What I didn't see yet was that proximity had quietly turned into dependency, and dependency always carries a cost. Over time, more of my energy went into managing complexity rather than shaping direction, and that shift happened gradually enough that it felt normal while it was happening.

This is the phase most leaders misread, and I did too. When growth slows without breaking, it's easy to assume the answer is to grind harder and push through. What I hadn't recognized yet was that the cost wasn't coming from a lack of work. It was coming from the growing gap between how the business had been built and what it now required to move forward. The signal wasn't a failure. It was compression.

By the time you feel it clearly, you've usually been paying for it longer than you realize.

As the dealerships grew and J&L continued to mature, I became increasingly dissatisfied with the results. Not because the business was failing, but because it had stopped moving the way it once did. We were profitable, stable, and respected, yet the growth no longer matched the effort. I wasn't confused about what needed attention and I wasn't short on ideas. What frustrated me was that pushing harder wasn't producing the same return, and the model that had carried us this far wasn't creating the momentum I expected at this stage. I could feel that the next constraint wasn't another operational fix or strategic tweak. It was how I was leading, how I was thinking, and what I was willing (or unwilling) to confront about myself.

Enter Jay Tepley. Jay helps men cut through drift, erase hidden blocks and gain clarity around their purpose. At the time, I didn't know I needed any of that. When her message landed in my LinkedIn inbox, something about it hit me. Normally I ignored messages like that. But her mission aligned with what I was feeling, even if I couldn't articulate it yet.

Responding to her message changed everything.

Our subsequent conversations pushed me into a level of introspection I had avoided for years. She challenged me to confront the fears, patterns, and beliefs I hid under the label of "I'm fine." She taught me how to look inward, not just talk about it. She made me take inventory of who I had become and who I was supposed to be.

What began as coaching turned into a two-week intense private training in Costa Rica that became a turning point in my life. In those two weeks, I uncovered truths I didn't know were buried: limiting beliefs, comfort zones, the old identity I had been protecting, and the future I was resisting without realizing it.

With her guidance, I gained clarity around my purpose, my faith, my direction, and the next chapter of my life. It led to a profound shift in how I worked and how I led, and eventually it led to the concept for the mastermind group, Me Plus Ultra.

It also allowed me to finally trust the strategic vision of someone who would guide J&L into its next era: Jamil Zabaneh (yes...the son of Jose). When he recommended pivoting from a large sales force to a client-first model focused on support, strategy and data, I resisted at first. After doing the deeper work with Jay though, I saw that holding on to what had worked in the past was the real danger. Letting go felt risky, but it was the only way forward.

Once I did, everything changed. Our growth skyrocketed. Client retention improved. Referrals multiplied. Our clients began seeing results three times higher than our competitors.

None of that happened because of tactics or because I became instantly smarter. It happened because I finally grew as a leader and let the right people challenge me.

Around that same period, another thread in my life was starting to form, one that didn't begin with systems or strategy, but with the relationships that would eventually reshape everything that came next.

What I didn't understand yet was that the shift I experienced in those rooms wasn't just about collaboration, it was about how relationships quietly redefine the way you lead. That's where the next chapter begins, but first an interlude.

Interlude: The First Spark

Before anything ever resembled a leadership retreat, it started with a friendship I didn't see coming. I first met Sandy Cerami at a business conference in 2018. He had been a past J&L client, but we never talked until that event. Afterward, he invited me to New York to be a guest on his podcast (the first podcast I had ever appeared on). We met for dinner the night before the recording and that dinner turned into a long conversation about business, leadership, and the patterns we both saw in entrepreneurs. We connected instantly and became close friends from that point forward.

When COVID hit in early 2020, Sandy and I started talking about how much anxiety and uncertainty our clients were dealing with. Many of them had businesses across multiple states, each with different restrictions and constantly changing rules. They were overwhelmed and had no idea what the best next move was. We decided the right thing to do (the only thing to do) was to help. No fees, no funnels, no strategy behind it. Just help.

We organized weekly Zoom calls and invited any business owner who needed support. We brought in lawyers, HR professionals, CPAs, sales experts, marketing experts - anyone who could offer clarity during a chaotic time. Those calls were open, collaborative, and grounded in one simple goal: give people the answers and perspectives they couldn't find anywhere else.

Sandy and I realized how much clarity came from those calls, so we started hosting our own weekly "happy hour business sessions." No agenda, no pressure, just two friends solving problems over a bourbon and cigar. Eventually we invited Jamil, and the conversations got even better.

This is what led to what became "The 4th Box" – a weekly invite for one additional leader to join us. No cost, no sales pitch, no hidden motive. Just real problem-solving with people who needed direction.

People loved it because those calls gave them something most leaders rarely get: a place to talk honestly and be fully understood.

And that's what planted the seed for what would come next.

The Expansion That Followed

Those weekly conversations showed us something important. When people are given a structured environment where they can be honest, think out loud, and work through real problems, the medium wasn't what made the difference. It was the way the room was built and the expectations we set for the people inside it.

As those sessions continued, we could feel something shifting. The conversations were becoming more strategic and more personal at the same time. There was a depth forming in those discussions that told us people were craving more than a weekly virtual touchpoint.

We started talking about what it might look like to take the momentum from our weekly calls and build something a little deeper. Not a replica of the 4th Box, but something that kept the parts that made those sessions so effective, the ease of the conversations and how often we left with more clarity than we expected. So we reached out to a small group of leaders we knew could contribute at a high level.

There was no brand yet, no event name, no agenda. The idea was simple: get a handful of people together and create more of the same energy that had been so valuable during a time when everyone was navigating uncertainty. The invitation reflected that simplicity, come share ideas, challenge each other, and at night we'll enjoy a bourbon and cigar.

Thirteen leaders showed up. It wasn't a conference or a production. It was a room full of people who were ready for real conversations, not the polished versions they were used to offering the world. The moment we sat down, I could tell most of them carried more strain than they were letting on.

Across two days, the conversations went exactly where they needed to go. People opened up, asked sharper questions, and pushed each other in ways that rarely happen in typical business settings. Ideas that felt stuck finally moved, and relationships began forming faster than I'd ever seen in a business environment.

By the time the retreat ended, people were already asking when the next one would take place. That was the moment it was obvious that this gathering wasn't a one-time experience, but the beginning of something that needed to be built with intention.

During those early days of the 4th Box and the first Business Bourbon & Cigars retreat, the idea for a different kind of mastermind began to take shape. I didn't have a formal plan yet, just a sense that the way leaders were thinking together in those rooms was the beginning of something bigger. Later, during my work with Jay Tepley, that loose idea finally developed into a clear framework built around collaboration, candor, and high-level decision-making. When I looked back at that very first retreat, it confirmed what I suspected: the concept wasn't theoretical. It worked. Those rooms gave the idea structure, identity, and the foundation it needed to grow into what would eventually become Me Plus Ultra.

Me Plus Ultra didn't start as a business idea. It started as a question I kept coming back to during those early retreats and 4th Box sessions: what would happen if there was a room where leaders could think together at the highest level... every month, not just during a crisis or a single event?

That question stayed with me because I knew exactly what had been missing throughout most of my career. I didn't need more content. I didn't need motivational speakers. I needed peers who told the truth, asked the right questions, and pushed me into decisions I had avoided. Those retreat conversations made it impossible to ignore how powerful that kind of room could be if it existed intentionally, not accidentally.

It wasn't something we set out to commercialize. It was to build an environment I wish I'd had twenty years earlier, something designed for leaders who weren't looking for inspiration as much as they were looking for clarity, accountability, and sharper thinking.

As it began to take shape, one thing became obvious: it couldn't be open to everyone. Not because of exclusivity, but because the room only works when people show up with honesty, ownership, and the willingness to challenge and be challenged. Over time we built a simple guardrail to protect that culture. Members nominate the people they believe belong beside them. It's not about volume; it's about making sure the room stays strong enough to do what it's designed to do.

The true origin of Me Plus Ultra isn't found in the logistics. It goes back to the realization that leaders think differently when the environment calls them to a higher standard. That's what those early sessions taught me. The forward traction didn't come from the platform or the format. It came from the people and what happened when they started thinking together honestly.

Me Plus Ultra grew out of that clarity, as a room built for leaders who want to think at the level they're capable of and grow at the pace their ambitions deserve.

I didn't have the language for it yet, but I was about to learn that relationships weren't a bonus — they were the lever.

The Moment Relationships Became the Strategy

02

In the past, I treated relationships like background noise, good to have, not a lever worth pulling. They were nice, sure, but not essential. I wasn't someone who walked into a room and tried to meet everybody. If I'm being honest, I avoided those rooms altogether whenever I could. I believed effort was the answer to everything. If something needed to be figured out, I'd figure it out. If there was a problem, I'd outwork it. That mindset got me pretty far, but it also built walls I didn't even realize I was living behind.

When I started my first podcast, *Move. Crush. Count.*, I still had one foot in J&L Marketing and one foot in whatever was coming next. Those early episodes make me cringe now, not because of the guests or the content, but because of how tightly I held myself. I wasn't truly listening. I was thinking about the next question I needed to ask, rehearsing lines in my head, trying to maintain some polished version of myself I thought the world expected. It was the introvert in me trying to perform instead of connect.

There was one moment that exposed just how much I was getting in my own way. A guest answered a question, then tossed a genuinely powerful question back to me and I completely missed it. I knew they had said something, but I had been so focused on the next thing I wanted to say that their question didn't even register. I fumbled through a response and hoped it didn't sound as awkward as it felt. Later, listening back, I heard the question clearly and it was one of those moments that could've made the entire episode better. But I wasn't present. I was more concerned with how I sounded than with who I was talking to.

That bothered me because I knew better. I told myself right then that if I was going to do this, I needed to show up — not the polished version of myself I thought people wanted, but the real one. The one who's curious, who cares about people, who wants to understand how things work and how people think. The moment I let go of trying to "perform," the podcast changed. And so did I.

Those small shifts were quietly training me for what followed. When we first started hosting Business Bourbon & Cigars retreats, I didn't know exactly what I was building. I just wanted a room where entrepreneurs could be honest, challenge each other, and stop pretending they had everything figured out.

But then something unexpected happened. After those first events, people kept coming up to me with this excitement in their voice. They'd tell me about someone they met, an idea they sparked together, an opportunity they never saw coming. Those conversations didn't stop when the event ended. They kept going. Weeks later, months later. Deals were happening. Collaborations were forming. People were becoming friends in a way that felt deeper than traditional networking.

Watching that happen changed me. It wasn't a gradual shift — it was almost instant. I felt myself opening up in ways I never had. I wanted to meet people. I wanted to know what they were building, what challenges they were facing, who I could connect them with. It felt natural, easy even, and that surprised me because nothing about "networking" had ever felt easy before.

My work with Jay would later help me understand why it clicked. Bringing people together, especially people with diverse skills and big vision, wasn't something I did accidentally. It was something I was wired for. I just didn't know it because I had spent so much of my early career trying to do everything myself. When I watched leaders in our rooms come together, leave their egos at the door, and genuinely try to help each other win, something in me shifted. Purpose snapped into place.

All of a sudden, I wasn't the introvert trying to survive the room. I was the connector building it.

The Strategic Power of the Right People

As our ecosystem grew, I started noticing something happening inside the group that I had never experienced in any other business setting.

When people feel safe enough to be honest and curious enough to help without any kind of agenda, the entire room starts operating on a different level.

Conversations deepen and new opportunities start to appear out of nowhere. Before long, things that normally take months or years to come together start happening in days, or even minutes.

One of the clearest examples of this came through one of our newest members, Alex Griffis, the president of Overfuel. When Alex joined, we treated him the same way we treat every leader who steps into this environment- we introduced him to people deliberately, not randomly. Not as a formality, but intentionally. For me, those introductions tie directly into the mission statement I live by: *bringing together visionary people with diverse skills so they can create breakthroughs together*. When you get the right mix of people in the right room, there's no ceiling for what can happen.

Not long after he joined, Alex participated in one of our Breakthrough Sessions. He came in holding onto a decision he'd been putting off, whether or not to make a six-figure investment that he wasn't fully confident in. You could tell he'd been wrestling with it for a while. That's the thing about big decisions: if you avoid them long enough, they start to feel heavier than they legitimately are. Sometimes all it takes is the right room to look at the problem with you.

As the group dug into his situation, people started asking the right questions. Not surface-level questions— real ones. The kind that forces clarity. Within minutes you could feel his thinking shift. By the time the session wrapped up, he had the answer he needed. He made the decision on the spot, and that choice put more than a hundred thousand dollars back in his pocket.

That however, wasn't even the moment that changed the trajectory of his business.

During that same conversation, Alex explained why scaling had been so difficult. Overfuel built exceptional websites and digital solutions for automotive clients, but many manufacturers in his industry use preferred vendor lists. If you're on one of those lists, the manufacturer helps offset the cost for the client. The savings can be massive— sometimes up to fifty percent. No matter how good your product is, if you're not on that list, you're fighting uphill.

Sitting in the session with Alex was Craig Misak. Craig had built a similar software solution for a large dealer group, and while it wasn't their core business, the software he developed had already earned preferred vendor status. They were looking to sell it because it was distracting them from their main focus.

As Alex talked through his challenge, I felt that familiar click in my head the moment something lines up so clearly you almost wonder how you didn't see it sooner. I knew Craig's group wanted to sell. I knew Alex needed preferred vendor status. I knew this wasn't coincidence. They were in the same room for a reason.

I introduced them immediately after the session.

They connected right away, and within six months, Overfuel acquired the software company. Because of that acquisition, they gained preferred vendor status overnight. The door that had been shut for years swung open instantly, and Alex wasted no time walking through it. Their client count exploded. Their opportunities multiplied. Their valuation climbed. Eventually I got a text from Alex that said, *"We're crushing it out here, SJ!"* and it came after a string of updates that made it clear he wasn't exaggerating.

That's the power of proximity. It compresses time, removes friction, and turns what "should take years" into something that happens over lunch.

The more I paid attention, the clearer it became: these weren't isolated wins they were early signs of what happens when the right people collide at the right moment.

This was just the beginning. The same thing happened at one of our leadership retreats in Scottsdale. Claudio Gambin, the Founder and CEO of GFG Solutions, was having a casual conversation with John Garcia, the founder of Solyco Capital. Claudio had a client who had just sold a real estate asset and was staring at a nine-million-dollar capital gains tax bill. John listened for a moment, asked a few questions, and mentioned a building owned by one of the companies Solyco had invested in. Claudio's client ended up purchasing the building through a 1031 exchange, eliminating the entire nine-million-dollar tax liability.

Claudio came up to me afterward, excited and almost in disbelief, and said, "We just saved a client nine million dollars."

Their partnership didn't end there. Today, GFG and Solyco have completed deals worth tens of millions of dollars, all because of one conversation at a lunch table.

None of that was scheduled or planned, and it certainly wasn't something we designed into the agenda. It was simply two people crossing paths at the exact moment one needed what the other had. For most of my life, I believed big opportunities required big planning. What I've learned is that they essentially require the right people. When you're in a room filled with the right relationships, ideas move faster, partnerships form without effort, and breakthroughs show up in places you'd never see on your own.

That's when it finally hit me: relationships weren't something extra or nice to have, they **were** the strategy.

What I didn't see yet was how much further that truth was about to go.

When the Room Became Something Bigger

As Me Plus Ultra continued to grow, the change showed up in ways I didn't anticipate. The deals and breakthroughs were impressive, but what was happening underneath all of that is what changed everything for me. There was a different kind of energy forming in these rooms. People were showing up for each other in ways that went well beyond business. Conversations felt more meaningful. Connections felt more intentional. I found myself watching it all unfold with this growing sense that the room was becoming more powerful than any agenda I could write.

That shift became impossible to ignore leading into Business Bourbon & Cigars 4, when Arnold Gacita, the President of Petra Automotive Products, called me and asked if he could bring someone he believed the room needed to meet. His guest was Troy Duhon, the owner of Premier Automotive Group and the founder of Giving Hope, a foundation committed to feeding families, building orphanages, and restoring dignity to people who'd been forgotten. Arnold had just come back from Brazil after helping Troy build one of those orphanages, and the experience had clearly changed him. There was a seriousness in his voice when he said, "Scott, I think the group should hear his story." I didn't know exactly what he meant yet, but I trusted Arnold enough to know it mattered.

We planned to bring Troy on stage the final morning, give him a few minutes, and keep the flow of the event intact. But that's not how the moment unfolded. Sometimes the room takes on a life of its own, and this was one of those nights. What happened next wasn't scheduled, and it wasn't prompted. It was one of those rare moments when the right person, the right story, and the right environment collide before anyone realizes what's happening.

That night we were on a rooftop terrace in Louisville, Kentucky. It was one of those evenings where everything just clicked. The mastermind sessions earlier in the day had everyone energized and fully engaged. By the time we reached the rooftop, the entire group was mingling, laughing, smoking cigars, sipping rare bourbons, and just enjoying being together. The conversations were rich. The networking didn't feel like networking; it felt like people genuinely trying to help each other.

So when Troy suddenly stepped onto a chair, the whole rooftop shifted. I didn't know where he was going with it, but I could feel the room pause just enough to sense something was about to happen. Up to that point, I had never heard him speak, and I don't usually like disrupting the momentum of a room that's flowing that well.

The second he opened his mouth, the entire tone of the night changed.

He shared a story about his father, about legacy, purpose, and what it essentially means to make an impact. Then he talked about his recent trip to Brazil with Arnold and the children they were helping. You could feel the room leaning in. The day had already been filled with breakthroughs, but this was different. The tone shifted. People weren't just listening, they were absorbing it.

Then, completely unexpectedly, he shifted to my father. Troy and my dad knew each other from the 90s, back when I had just started J&L. They were both part of a Toyota 20 Group — twenty dealers and managers from around the country who met to share best practices and hold each other accountable. My dad was the general manager at Green Tree Toyota. Troy owned his own Toyota store. They respected each other long before I ever built anything worth talking about, which made what happened next hit even harder. He began sharing things my father had said about me, things I had never heard before. Hearing those words in that setting from someone my father trusted, stopped me cold. I had to turn away for a moment just to pull myself together. It wasn't sadness... it was one of those moments that lands with a weight you feel before you fully understand it.

When Troy finished, the rooftop was silent. People were crying. Others were holding back tears. It was one of the most powerful five-minute moments I've ever witnessed in any room, business or otherwise.

Later that year, Arnold invited me to the Giving Hope gala in New Orleans. It was the first Giving Hope gala I had ever attended. He hosted a sponsor table and asked me to join him. After the event, he brought me into a smaller gathering, and to my surprise, I walked into the room and immediately recognized seven Me Plus Ultra members — Troy, Arnold, Dean Powery, Chuck Kramer, Brady Schmidt, Jorge Gomez, and myself. Some of the same people who felt moved on that rooftop were now showing up to support not only the mission, but each other.

We ended up around a table talking about the night, the cause, and the responsibility that comes with having the ability to help. At one point, I said that attending the gala was great, but we could do more. We had people in the group who genuinely cared. We had entrepreneurs who weren't just successful — they had the heart and the desire to use their success for something significant.

Right there at that table, the idea of hosting Giving Hope auctions at our leadership retreats was born.

In just the first three years, Me Plus Ultra members raised over one million dollars for Giving Hope — and that alone would have been enough to be proud of. But what stayed with me wasn't the money. It was what started happening afterward. As members built deeper relationships and learned more about each other's lives and missions, they didn't just support Giving Hope, they began showing up for the causes that mattered to the people in the room. That's how several members became involved with Arnold's charitable organization, Petra Cares. Others stepped in to support initiatives like Big Brothers Big Sisters or needs they learned about through the group. These weren't casual donations or polite gestures. They were genuine acts of support born from real connection.

A few years later, I attended the Petra Cares Gala. As the evening unfolded, I started noticing something I wasn't expecting. I'd look across the room and recognize someone... then another... then another. Before long, nearly ten percent of the people at the gala were members from our mastermind group — not because of me, but because they believed in Arnold and believed in the Petra Cares mission.

Several members came up to me that night and said some version of, "Look at what has happened because we all met each other." They were right. What began as a mastermind was becoming something much bigger, a circle of leaders who genuinely want to see each other win in business and in life.

This wasn't just a community being built. I was organically upgrading my collaborating circle, and my core circle, and I didn't even recognize it until I stood in that room and saw the impact for myself.

The business wins were impressive. The people were what made the room matter.

When the Truth Finally Shows Up

The deeper shift didn't come from the deals or the causes. It came from what started happening in the conversations themselves.

As powerful as the business breakthroughs were, something deeper started happening in these rooms, something I didn't fully recognize at first. It wasn't loud or dramatic, and it didn't happen all at once, but it was real. Little by little, the conversations began shifting from what people were comfortable saying to what they really needed to say. When I look back now, that shift may have been the most important part of everything we were building.

Most leaders don't walk into a room ready to expose what's in fact going on inside their business. They start with the answers that feel safest, the ones that sound responsible and polished. I'd hear things like, "I need help scaling," or, "My sales team isn't performing the way it should," or, "We need to refine our processes." They're not lying. Those problems are real. They're just not the whole truth. They're what you share before you trust the room enough to say what's keeping you up at night.

But when the environment is right, when people genuinely want to help, when there's no competition for status, when there's no reason to impress anyone, leaders start saying the things they've been carrying alone for a long time. Not because they suddenly want to, but because they finally feel like they can.

That's when you hear what's truly keeping them up at night.

"My company is growing, but internally it feels chaotic."
"I'm burned out and pretending everything is fine."
"I don't have the processes people think I do."
"I feel like I'm guessing more than leading."
"I'm afraid to make the wrong decision because everything is on the line."

When someone finally says something like that out loud, you can feel the room shift. There's this moment where the surface-level talk falls away and the real work begins. What always struck me was how the group responded. Nobody judged them. Nobody pulled back. If anything, people leaned in closer. They wanted to understand. They wanted to help, and the more that happened, the more honest the conversations became.

I realized quickly that people don't hide their real problems because they're weak, they hide them because they're alone. When a leader doesn't have a room they trust, they build walls. They create polished versions of their challenges, hoping those versions are enough to get by. The right room makes those walls unnecessary. You see someone exhale when they finally say what's specifically going on. Not because the problem has been solved yet, but because the burden is finally shared.

As I watched this happen, it changed the way I thought about leadership altogether. I started paying closer attention to the questions people **weren't** asking and the truths they were dancing around. I found myself listening differently, listening for what someone meant instead of what they said. The more honest people became, the more clarity emerged. Solutions that felt impossible on their own suddenly became obvious when the truth was finally on the table.

It was in those moments that I understood something I had missed for most of my career. Relationships weren't just about opportunity. They were about access. Access to better thinking, better decisions, better clarity. Access to truth. In business, truth is one of the most valuable assets you can have, because you can't solve what you're unwilling to name or accept.

I used to believe leadership was about having the answers. Now, I know it's about putting yourself in rooms where the right questions get asked, rooms where you aren't expected to pretend, rooms where you can admit what's real without wondering how it will look, rooms where the truth finally shows up and does what it's supposed to do.

Looking back, the breakthroughs, deals, and opportunities were impressive, but none of those things were the foundation. The foundation was trust, the kind that only forms when people stop performing and start being honest. Once I understood that, I could see my own journey more clearly. I wasn't just hosting rooms, I was learning from them. The more I leaned into that truth, the more the rooms transformed me, too.

The Breakthrough I Couldn't Have Reached Alone

As consequential as all these moments were, the biggest shift didn't show up in the form of a deal, partnership, or a charity initiative. It showed up in how I started thinking. The more time I spent in rooms filled with people who challenged my assumptions, asked better questions, and pushed each other to see around corners, the more my own thinking began to evolve. I wasn't just learning from the group, I was being shaped by it.

These moments showed me how relationships expand your heart. What came next showed me how they expand your thinking.

It would've been easy to assume moments like that were rare, but what surprised me even more was how often the room was reshaping me in ways I didn't see coming.

This became unmistakable during one of our expert sessions on AI. We were deep into a conversation about where technology was heading, how quickly industries were shifting, and what opportunities might appear for the people who were ready. One of our members, Mark Queen, asked a simple, but sharp question, and it hit me like a jolt. It wasn't just the question itself; it was the way the room had been building toward it, the way the dialogue had been stretching my thinking in directions I wouldn't have gone on my own.

Before the session even ended, I started testing the idea in the room. Dave Boyle was one of the first people I turned to. Dave had been with us since that very first retreat with thirteen people, and over the years he's become one of my closest friends, someone with a rare instinct for the marketplace and a way of seeing angles most people miss. Sandy Cerami was right there with us too, absorbing the conversation and sharpening it in real time, the same way he has in dozens of conversations we've had over the years. The three of us talked through what the idea could look like, where it might break, and what would have to be true for it to work. Those early reactions didn't just validate the idea; they shaped it in ways I never would have gotten to on my own.

By the time those conversations wrapped, the idea had taken shape so clearly that it almost felt too obvious. It was the kind of idea that could completely disrupt a major legacy industry, one that, if executed correctly, could scale to levels I had never imagined, and the crazy part? Five years earlier, I wouldn't have believed I was capable of building something like it. I would have thought it was too big, too technical, too complicated. I would have shrugged it off and said, "Someone should invent that."

This time, I didn't think that. This time, I thought, "I can do this."

That shift had nothing to do with confidence and everything to do with relationships.

At this point in my life, I wasn't trying to figure everything out alone. I was surrounded by people who had built billion-dollar organizations, people who understood capital, technology, scaling, fundraising, and execution at levels I had never operated at yet. I had people I could call who would challenge my assumptions, poke holes in my thinking, and guide me toward what was essentially possible — not just what felt comfortable.

So I started moving. Within three days, I had a full business plan drafted. Within weeks, I was in conversations with people who could help execute it. Over the following months, the plan evolved into something far more sophisticated than what I originally imagined- larger in scope, more refined and more powerful.

Every step of the way, the right people helped shape it. They helped pressure test the idea. They helped identify blind spots. They helped refine how we should enter the market. They helped clarify the revenue model, the technology stack, the operational requirements and the roadmap.

The more the idea grew, the more one truth became impossible to ignore: **I never would have reached this breakthrough on my own.**

Not because I lacked the intelligence or the drive, but because innovation rarely shows up in isolation. It shows up when the right people ask the right questions in the right room.

Looking back now, I can see how all of this tied together: the shift from introvert to connector, the breakthroughs I witnessed in others, the conversations that turned into opportunities, the moments that expanded from business into something far more profound. All of it pointed to the same conclusion:

I had spent years trying to succeed by doing everything myself, and the ceiling on that approach was far lower than I ever realized. The moment I stopped trying to be the entire engine and started surrounding myself with people who thought differently, saw differently, and operated differently, the ceiling disappeared.

That's when it finally became clear: **Relationships weren't just a strategy. They were the environment everything else depended on.**

Their real value wasn't in making business easier, it was in expanding what I believed was possible. They expose blind spots you don't know you have. They accelerate ideas you couldn't refine alone. They pull the truth out of you when you're avoiding it. They reveal opportunities that simply don't exist when you try to build everything from inside your own head.

For most of my early career, I believed success came from effort, discipline, and focus. Those things definitely matter, but they aren't the differentiator. The differentiator is the environment you choose and the people you allow into it. In other words, the rooms you participate in.

Over time, it became clear that an AI breakthrough wasn't the real breakthrough. The real breakthrough was understanding that the right relationships had fundamentally changed what I believed was possible- not just for my business, but for myself.

Once you experience that shift, the question changes, it stops being "How do I make this work?" and becomes, "What room makes this inevitable?"

That's when everything changes.

The Reality Behind Masterminds

03

Throughout this book, the language shifts intentionally. "Mastermind" refers to a format or label people recognize in the market. When I use "room" and "environment," I'm referring to where the real work of thinking, challenge, and decision-making actually happens. What ultimately matters isn't the label attached to the gathering, but the standard the environment enforces and the pressure it applies. Some formats never rise to that level. That distinction only became clear to me after experiencing both sides of it.

By the time I started taking a serious look at mastermind groups, I already had a reference point for what real collaboration felt like. I had been in a room where people spoke plainly, challenged each other without posturing, and worked through real issues instead of rehearsing answers. I didn't fully understand why that experience mattered at the time, but it quietly set a standard I would measure everything else against.

That's why what happened next was so jarring.

As I evaluated and joined groups that labeled themselves as masterminds, I assumed they were built on the same principles. The language sounded familiar. The promises were similar. The positioning suggested depth, honesty, and collective problem-solving. But once inside, the difference was obvious. These rooms didn't operate the way I expected, not because the people were unqualified or the intentions were bad, but because the structure itself didn't support the kind of interaction that directly produces breakthroughs.

That contrast is why I looked closer at what was happening. The problem wasn't effort. It wasn't intelligence. It wasn't even commitment. It was something more fundamental. Most masterminds weren't failing because the people inside them were doing something wrong, they were failing because of how the rooms were designed in the first place.

When Structure Quietly Dilutes Capability

Most masterminds fail for a simple reason: the people in the room never directly work together. They share updates that feel safe, not realities that would essentially help the room understand what's going on. They talk about symptoms instead of root causes, and because the dialogue never gets below the surface, the room has no chance of producing a real breakthrough.

I saw that pattern repeat across multiple groups. They had strong branding, compelling messaging, and smart people leading them, but the structure never supported meaningful participation. People weren't avoiding honesty because they lacked courage, they avoided it because the environment didn't invite it. Without trust, the conversations stay shallow.

It reminded me of watching a sports team practice without pressure. Everything looks coordinated from a distance, but nothing holds up once the real game starts. You can't prepare for high stakes in a low-stakes environment. You can't create breakthrough thinking in a room where no one is willing, or structurally encouraged, to say what the reality is.

The groups I joined weren't short on intelligence or ambition. The limitation was design. They weren't built to create collaboration, they were built to deliver content, and those are two entirely different outcomes.

A Live Example of Structural Failure

One moment made the issue impossible to ignore. I belonged to a group a few years ago and joined a "mastermind call" with several hundred other members. The host gave a short message and opened the Q&A. Instantly, the chat filled with questions, real questions about real problems. You could tell people were genuinely looking for help.

Almost none of those questions were addressed.

Only the simplest ones were selected, answered quickly, and the rest were moved past. There was no dialogue, exploration, or opportunity for anyone else in the group to contribute. When the call ended, all the energy and curiosity in the chat went with it. Nothing stuck.

Sitting there afterward, it was clear why the experience felt so empty. The issue wasn't the people, the leader or even the content. The problem was the way the room was built. There was no mechanism for members to think together, no expectation of participation, no structure that encouraged people to speak honestly, and no form of accountability that pushed conversations beyond the surface. Without those things, trust doesn't form. Without trust, breakthroughs don't happen. The room wasn't designed to create transformation; it was designed to deliver information. It was a presentation with an audience, not a mastermind.

Once I understood that, the gaps in every other group became obvious.

Why Trust Is a Structural Requirement, Not a Value

A real mastermind isn't defined by a charismatic leader, an immaculate curriculum, or an impressive guest list. Those things may add value, but they don't create transformation. The real engine is trust. Trust is created by the structure of the room, not by motivational language or marketing.

You can see a version of this in great sports organizations. Think of a team reviewing game film. No one sugarcoats anything. They pause the playback, rewind it, call out mistakes, and work together to solve them. Not because anyone enjoys being wrong, but because the standard is winning and the team is committed to improving. The structure of that environment demands honesty. It invites accountability. It produces growth.

Masterminds are supposed to operate the same way. Most don't.

Most rooms never get beyond polite updates or surface-level discussion because the people inside them haven't been given a structure that makes trust possible. Without trust, the room stays flat. Flat rooms don't challenge your assumptions, expose your blind spots, or help you solve the problems you're too close to see clearly.

Once I recognized how essential trust was, not as a soft concept, but as an operational requirement, the differences between strong and weak rooms became easy to see. The strong ones weren't built around a personality. They were built around the members. The breakthroughs didn't come from the front of the room. They came from across it.

Without trust, a mastermind is just an event. With trust, it becomes a catalyst for exponential thinking.

Once you see how much trust determines what a room can actually produce, it's tempting to believe the difference between strong and weak environments should be obvious. What complicates that judgment is that capable leaders often experience weak rooms differently, not because the structure works, but because their own strength compensates for what the room lacks.

How Strong Leaders End Up Carrying Weak Rooms

Most leaders don't stay in ineffective environments because they can't see the limitations. They stay because those limitations don't register as problems from the inside. The people are capable, the conversations sound intelligent, and progress continues just enough to justify staying put. Nothing feels urgent enough to force a serious question about whether the room itself is still doing any meaningful work.

Highly capable leaders are especially good at adapting to imperfect conditions. When conversations stay vague, they translate them into action later. When decisions don't fully close, they carry the responsibility forward themselves. When momentum slows, they create it. Over time, that adaptability stops being an advantage and starts becoming a blind spot. Because they can compensate, the environment never has to improve, and its weaknesses stay hidden.

This is how competence creates tolerance for inefficiency. Leaders who know how to operate under pressure don't need the room to function well in order to produce results. They pull out what's useful, leave the rest behind, and keep moving. Outcomes still happen, which makes it easy to believe the environment is contributing more than it really is. The room feels productive because capable people are productive inside it.

Prior success makes that distortion harder to catch. Leaders who have built something meaningful learn that urgency isn't always the answer and that patience often pays off. That instinct works well in execution and quietly undermines evaluation. Instead of asking whether the environment is sharpening their thinking, they ask whether it's actively causing harm. As long as nothing appears broken, staying the same feels like the responsible choice.

The effect is amplified when a leader becomes one of the stronger voices in the room. Their framing lands, their input carries weight, and others look to them for direction. That response feels validating, but it subtly changes the environment. Rather than challenging that leader's thinking, the room starts leaning on it. Stability replaces elevation, and the environment appears effective because strong individuals are holding it together.

Over time, cause and effect reverse. Instead of the environment improving the quality of thinking inside it, the most capable people become the reason it doesn't stall completely. Their competence fills structural gaps and smooths over weaknesses that would otherwise surface. Progress is replaced with things that are familiar, and consistency starts to be mistaken for growth.

Loyalty and patience usually enter at this stage without being named. Time has been invested, relationships have been built and the rhythm of the room feels familiar. Leaving seems unnecessary because nothing has failed outright, and it feels premature because the leader can still operate effectively inside the environment. What often goes unspoken is that patience is now protecting an identity that still works. The leader remains respected, productive and capable, which makes it difficult to admit that the room no longer asks anything new of them.

This is where functioning starts to get confused with working. Meetings continue, conversations sound thoughtful, and incremental progress shows up slowly enough to justify staying. Because the machine is still running, no decision feels urgent. What rarely gets examined is whether the environment is producing sharper thinking or simply allowing existing strengths to coast.

The most misleading signal is that everything still works. Businesses operate, decisions get made, and from the outside there's no obvious cost to remaining where things are. The cost shows up more quietly, in the compression that never happens, the assumptions that never get tested, and the timing that stretches without anyone noticing. Capable leaders absorb that cost without immediate consequence, which is exactly why these environments hold them for so long.

That's how strong leaders remain in rooms that no longer elevate them. Not because they lack ambition or awareness, but because their capability allows them to survive conditions that should otherwise force a decision. The signal isn't failure or dysfunction. It's the absence of pressure where pressure should exist, and that absence is hardest to notice when you're strong enough to carry the weight yourself.

Once that pattern becomes obvious, the way rooms get evaluated has to change. Appearance, history and reputation stop mattering as much as what the environment actually demands from the people inside it, and whether it applies pressure where growth is supposed to happen.

Designing a Room That Could Actually Hold the Work

When all of this finally clicked, I realized I wasn't looking for a better version of what was already out there. I was looking for something that didn't exist in the form I needed. I wanted a room where high-level leaders could be honest. A room where people were expected to contribute. A room where the thinking in the room was stronger than the thinking of any one person in it.

That became the foundation for Me Plus Ultra:
- The members are the asset.
- The room is the engine.
- The structure is what makes trust possible.

Me Plus Ultra wasn't built to follow trends or imitate anyone else's model. It was built because the type of environment I needed and the type high-level leaders thrive in wasn't being offered anywhere. A room designed for collaboration, built around trust, where people don't just talk about problems, they work on them together.

Once you experience a room like that, you understand why most groups fall short, and why the right room has the power to change the trajectory of your business and your life.

Why Environments Outperform Effort

04

For years, I believed my limits were tied to my abilities, how well I solved problems, how hard I worked, and how much experience I had accumulated. That belief held up until I stepped into a room filled with leaders running companies far larger than mine.

I expected to hear conversations about issues way above my pay grade. Instead, I heard the same challenges I was dealing with: hiring, retaining great people, eliminating friction, strengthening client experience, managing growth without breaking the business. The scale was different, but the problems were surprisingly familiar.

What changed wasn't the difficulty of the problems, it was the quality of the environment in which those problems were being solved. These leaders weren't surrounded by people who reinforced their assumptions. They were surrounded by people who sharpened their thinking. That was the difference.

For the first time, I had to admit something I hadn't been willing to confront. I wasn't limited by skill. I was limited by the rooms I stayed in. When you spend too much time being the one who solves everything, you don't realize how long you've gone without being challenged yourself. It's like lifting the same amount of weight for years, your form may improve, but your strength doesn't.

Part of why this went unnoticed is because I had already surpassed the life I once imagined for myself. Success can make comfort feel like wisdom. You stop asking bigger questions. You protect what you've built. You quiet the part of you that knows you're capable of more.

Why Hard Work Stops Producing New Growth

In the early years of a company, hard work can solve nearly anything. Problems are smaller, cycles are shorter, and progress responds directly to effort. As a business grows, the mechanics change long before the leader realizes it.

That's what happened at J&L. When growth slowed, I did what had always worked: I pushed harder, worked more hours, had more pressure, as well as personal involvement. The business wasn't small anymore though. The problems weren't simple, effort didn't move the needle the way it used to.

The business had grown vastly more complex, more clients, more people, more moving parts. I was still treating it like the version I once started with, where being hands-on was the advantage. *At scale*, that same instinct becomes a bottleneck. *What once sped things up now slowed everything down.*

At the same time, the demands on me as a leader changed. Early on, success rewards intensity. Later, the game shifts toward clarity, direction, and the ability to make decisions without being involved in everything. The problem was, I was still operating as if intensity alone could compensate for uncertainty.

There was also a personal dimension I hadn't acknowledged. I was wrestling privately with what I wanted my next chapter to be. I hadn't lost interest in the business, but I didn't have the same sense of direction I'd once had. When a leader's identity becomes blurry, the organization feels it long before the leader admits it.

So there I was, managing a more complex business with the same tools I used years earlier, without the clarity needed to see the real issues. Hard work didn't fix anything. It amplified the wrong things. I became more reactive, more frustrated, and more controlling in an attempt to regain traction. None of it worked.

The real problem wasn't effort. It was that the business had evolved, and I hadn't evolved with it. The tools that built the company couldn't carry it into its next phase. Hard work wasn't the lever anymore. New insight was. That insight didn't appear until I put myself in environments where the assumptions I'd been operating under were no longer sufficient.

When Effort Stops Compounding

There's a version of effort that looks productive on the surface but quietly signals that something underneath has stopped working.

It doesn't show up as laziness or disengagement. It shows up as volume, more activity, more communication, and a level of coordination that feels heavier than it should for work the team already knows how to do.

Meetings multiply first. Not because people enjoy them, but because alignment no longer holds cleanly between conversations. Decisions that once traveled without friction now require extra time and attention to stay intact. A meeting that used to resolve an issue now schedules another, not to move the work forward, but to make sure nothing drifts between sessions. Calendars fill, not with new initiatives, but with work designed to keep existing decisions from unraveling.

Follow-ups become more deliberate. Leaders recap conversations that once ended with clear ownership. Deadlines get restated. Expectations are clarified again. None of this feels inefficient in the moment. It feels careful and responsible, like what leadership requires when the stakes are high and you're trying to keep things clean.

As coordination costs rise, the system compensates. Activity that once moved through the organization with minimal friction starts routing around pressure points. More people are included, not because their input is essential, but because certainty has weakened. Decisions take longer to settle because conversations become more thorough without always becoming final, leaving work slightly unfinished even after it's been discussed.

Eventually, senior leaders feel the shift in their own workload. They step back into execution- not because they want to- but because it's faster than waiting for alignment to work its way through the system. They review work that shouldn't need review. They stay in conversations they shouldn't need to be involved in. Small decisions start flowing back upward because the overhead of coordination has grown heavier than the decisions themselves. It doesn't register as failure; it registers as necessary.

When effort compounds, decisions hold. When it doesn't, leaders stay involved just to keep decisions intact. Progress still shows up, but it demands attention that wasn't there previously.

This is where capable leaders misdiagnose the problem. Structure gets layered on top of structure. Communication expands to cover gaps that clarity once handled on its own. Oversight increases, not as control, but as insurance. Each move makes sense in isolation, but together they signal that the environment is no longer carrying its share of the work.

Effort was never meant to replace an environment. It was meant to be amplified by it. When the environment weakens, effort gets consumed just keeping things upright. Since strong leaders can shoulder that load for a long time, the cost stays hidden until exhaustion, delay, or missed opportunity finally forces the question that should have been asked earlier.

The Myth of the Self-Made Leader

In the beginning, self-reliance feels like a superpower. You build something from nothing. You push through barriers. You keep going when most people stop. At a certain point though, the same instinct that drove your early success becomes the thing holding you back.

I began seeing this during the period when Sandy and I spoke regularly. Those conversations weren't about motivation, they were about expanding the available options. He'd challenge something I said, introduce a different angle, or point out a blind spot I didn't even know I had. It wasn't that I lacked answers. I lacked someone to challenge the answers I was defaulting to.

Then came the moment with Jamil. He didn't dance around it. He looked at me and said, "Scott, you have a brand problem." He wasn't talking about J&L or any of my companies, he was talking about me. I was stretched across so many roles and projects that nobody, including myself, could clearly articulate who I was as a leader or where I was heading. I hadn't become unclear because I lacked direction; I had become unclear because I hadn't stopped long enough to decide who I wanted to be next. His insight exposed a part of leadership nobody talks about: success can dilute your identity if you never redefine it.

Jay's initial message drove this point home even more. She described the internal tension I had been ignoring with uncomfortable accuracy: successful, but stalled; accomplished, but uncertain; driven, but without a defined horizon. She didn't tell me what to do. She simply reflected what I had been unwilling to acknowledge.

Self-made leaders aren't the ones who do everything themselves. They're the ones who recognize when their own view has become the constraint. The ceiling they hit isn't effort, it's the absence of outside challenge.

Why You Don't Think Bigger Alone

I saw this pattern repeat itself again when it came to ideas. Big ideas rarely come from isolation. They come from the friction created when someone else challenges the way you see a problem. Left alone, your thinking loops through the same patterns. Your brain reuses the same assumptions. *You reach the edges of your imagination long before you reach the edges of your potential.*

The original concept felt solid, ambitious, clear, and well-structured, but once I brought in people whose strengths filled my blind spots, everything opened up.

They weren't adding noise. They were revealing dimensions of the idea I couldn't see on my own. Someone would ask a question that shifted the frame. Someone else would point out an opportunity hidden inside the original structure. Another person would challenge the limits I had quietly built around the idea without realizing it.

It was like looking at a landscape through a small window and suddenly having someone widen the frame. The terrain didn't change. My awareness of it did.

That's why you can't think bigger alone. Not because you lack creativity or courage, but because every idea is shaped by the limits of the person holding it. When the room expands, the idea expands. When the idea expands, so does the leader.

Elite Rooms: The Accelerators You Never Knew You Needed

Some environments change you without announcing themselves as transformational. Monterey Car Week became one of those environments for me. On the surface, it's an automotive event, but it attracts people who think at an altitude that forces you to rethink your own assumptions about what's possible.

The conversations aren't formal. They happen around fire pits, over lunch in Carmel, or walking the grounds at The Quail. The openness is what makes them powerful. People talk honestly about decisions they struggled with, risks they took, the times they nearly chose the wrong path, and the lessons that reshaped their careers.

Nobody is posturing. Nobody is hiding. They aren't sharing to impress; they're sharing because they understand that the right insight at the right time can compress years of struggle into a moment of clarity.

Being around leaders who think that way resets your internal yardstick. You stop assuming your challenges are unique. You stop believing your opportunities are capped. You begin evaluating decisions the way they do, through a broader lens, with more confidence and less hesitation.

Those trips didn't hand me opportunities. They sharpened my ability to recognize them. They made me more curious, more decisive, and more willing to question limits I had accepted without realizing it.

Five years ago, I thought my entrepreneurial run was winding down. Today, I'm as energized and engaged as I was in my twenties (maybe more), but this time the work has deeper meaning. That shift didn't come from effort. It came from putting myself in these environments where bigger thinking was normal, and where the expectations were high enough to pull me forward.

The right rooms don't inflate your ego. They recalibrate your vision. Once that happens, growth stops being an aspiration and becomes the only direction.

The Anatomy of a Better Room

05

When I say "room," I'm talking about any environment where leaders sit together to think, solve problems, and challenge each other. A peer group, leadership team, workshop, or a mastermind. The label doesn't matter. What matters is how the room functions. By this point in the book, we've already covered *why* the right room matters; now we're shifting to something more practical- how to recognize one.

Strong rooms are built on specific mechanics. They're not complicated, but they're easy to overlook until you've been in a room that does them well. The composition, expectations, level of preparation, and standards all determine whether a room unlocks breakthroughs or quietly holds you in place. A poorly structured room might look impressive from the outside, but on the inside it feels like trying to tune a guitar with worn-out strings; you can keep tuning and adjusting, but it never holds the note. A well-structured room, on the other hand, stays in tune. Every person contributes, the problem converts into decisions, and progress is made.

Mastermind groups are simply one version of a room, they're built with more intention, more structure, and a clearer operating rhythm than most. But the traits we're about to walk through apply to every setting where leaders work together. If these elements are there, the room helps you think and perform at a higher level. If they're missing, the room limits you, even if the people inside it are talented.

In the next few pages, I'm going to show you the key elements of a room built for quality outcomes.

The Three Forces That Shape Leaders: People, Pressure, Perspective

The people in the room determine the ceiling. If everyone comes in with the same lens, assumptions, or way of solving problems, the room eventually hits a ceiling. I'm not saying industry-specific rooms can't be great, some of the best rooms I joined early in my career were built around a single industry, and they were exactly what I needed at that stage. But as you grow, the limitations of single-lens thinking start to show up. Eventually, you need people who don't see the world the way you do. That's where the breakthroughs come from.

Pressure- when it's healthy- reinforces intelligence. Good pressure shows up when everyone is prepared, engaged, and serious about helping the person in the spotlight. When the room operates that way, the standard rises automatically, no one wants to be the weak link. The pressure itself isn't the problem. It's the structure underneath it. When glass and diamond are both exposed to pressure, one cracks, the other sharpens. Bad pressure makes people shrink, hold back, or worry about how they look. Strong rooms eliminate that by design.

Perspective is the force that accelerates growth. Someone from a completely different world can look at your situation and point to the thing you've avoided, ignored, missed, or justified. They don't carry your assumptions. They're not tied to your identity or your past decisions. They can see a clearer picture. When a room has enough diversity of experience, those moments happen often, and they change how you think going forward.

Those three forces (people, pressure, and perspective) are what shape leaders over time, but they only work when the room is built to support them. Without trust, people stay guarded and protect themselves instead of attacking the real issue. Without standards, pressure loses its edge and turns into background noise. Without accountability, perspective never turns into action and insights die on the table. What follows aren't additional forces layered on top of the original three; they're the conditions that allow those forces to function the way they're supposed to.

What a Strong Room Does in the First Ten Minutes

In the opening minutes, a strong room establishes what the purpose actually is. The issue isn't introduced as context or background; it's framed around a decision or constraint that has to move. Someone names what needs to change, what's blocking it right now, and what the room is being asked to help resolve. The conversation doesn't warm up by circling the topic. It starts by locking the target.

General language doesn't last long. When someone speaks in broad terms, the room narrows it immediately. Questions come back that force precision: *What's the exact point of friction right now? What hasn't moved despite effort? What decision needs to be closed before this ends?* The intent isn't to sound sharp or prove a point. It's to keep the discussion from drifting into interpretation instead of tangible actions.

The conversation doesn't move forward in stronger rooms until the language does. If the issue can't be stated cleanly, the conversation doesn't advance. Not because anyone is being difficult, but because the room understands that ambiguity compounds faster than insight if it's allowed to linger.

Trust: The Foundation of Transformational Rooms

Trust is the foundation that makes every other part of the room work. Without trust, people protect their reputation instead of attacking the problem. They share partial truths. They soften what they're dealing with. They offer safe answers instead of honest ones. Once the information is incomplete, everything else falls apart, questions get weaker, insights become generic, and solutions never hit the real issue.

Rooms with strong trust operate differently. People say the thing they've been avoiding. They put the real numbers on the table. They admit when something isn't working. They talk about the decisions they're unsure about. Once that level of honesty becomes normal, the quality of the session jumps. You're no longer working on symptoms; you're addressing the root and once you solve the real problem, everything else becomes easier.

Trust isn't created by speeches or promises. It's created by confidentiality, consistency, and behavior, the things that signal to everyone in the room: "You're safe to tell the truth here."

Standards:
Why High Expectations Produce Breakthroughs

High standards aren't about being perfect; they're about protecting the room from mediocrity. In strong rooms, preparation is non-negotiable. If someone is in the spotlight, they come with full context, clarity, and an actual ask. The people helping them come prepared, too. They've reviewed the material, thought through the issue, and are ready to contribute. Once the session starts, people show up fully present. No phones. No distractions. No half-in, half-out behavior.

Average rooms tolerate the opposite. Late arrivals, vague thinking, sloppy preparation, and weak follow-through. Those things erode the room over time. People stop giving their best thinking because they've learned it won't be used. Elite rooms don't allow that pattern to develop. Their standards create an environment where people take the work seriously, not because they have to, but because that's simply how the room operates.

Perspective Diversity: Seeing What You Can't See Alone

Rooms that lack diversity of thought eventually recycle the same ideas. You hear the same solutions framed ten different ways, but nothing fundamentally new. When the room includes people who see the world through different lenses (operators, strategists, financial minds, technical thinkers) you start uncovering angles you didn't know existed. The problem becomes clearer, the solutions sharper, and the thinking stronger.

This is also why so many breakthroughs come from people outside an industry. They're not conditioned by the industry's blind spots. They see gaps insiders overlook. Strong rooms replicate that advantage intentionally. They mix perspectives so members don't get trapped in one way of thinking.

Accountability: The Engine of Elite Growth

Accountability keeps the room from becoming a place where interesting ideas are shared and forgotten. In strong rooms, when you say something matters, the group expects you to act like it matters. When you commit to something, the expectation is simple: follow through. When you don't, it affects more than your progress, it affects group trust and culture.

Builders thrive in this environment. They execute quickly. They report back honestly. They turn insights into action. Performers struggle because they want the attention without the responsibility. They dominate conversations, protect their ego, or disappear when it's time to implement. The room exposes those patterns immediately.

Accountability keeps the room aligned. It's not about policing. It's about making sure people don't waste each other's time or compromise the integrity of the room because once that happens, even strong groups start to look like all the others. That's also why accountability alone isn't enough.

Why Better Rooms Have a Process

Rooms that rely on spontaneous conversation rarely solve meaningful problems. They produce opinions, not clarity. A room designed to create breakthroughs needs process, not rigid control, but a structure that keeps the thinking focused and the work relevant.

The pre-work matters because most people misdiagnose their own problems. Someone might show up saying, "Our salespeople need better follow-up," but once the room starts asking questions, it becomes obvious the real issue is that no one agreed on what a qualified opportunity actually looks like or a business owner might think their challenge is client retention, but with more context it becomes clear their onboarding process is inconsistent and confusing. This is why the pre-work isn't administrative, it's diagnostic. When the room walks in already understanding the mission, the background, and the outcome someone wants, the dialogue and analysis starts at a completely different level.

Think of it like taking a car to a mechanic and saying, "It makes a weird noise." At that point, they're guessing. Give them more detail (when it happens, under what conditions, what you were doing at the time) and the guesses get better, but they're still guesses. The moment you give them precise inputs, the uncertainty drops and the real issue shows up fast. Rooms should operate the same way. The clearer and more specific the surrounding details, the less time the group spends guessing and the faster it gets to the actual fix.

Once the session begins, structure keeps the room aligned. We start by making sure everyone is looking at the same picture, not different versions of the story. Clarifying questions come next, the kind that force specificity and expose what's being avoided. Questions like, "What decision did you postpone that led to this?" or "Where does this break every single time?" or "Who owns this today — not in theory, but in practice?" Sometimes it's as direct as, "What are you not saying because it's uncomfortable?" Those questions surface the real issue fast. Only then do solutions matter. Once options are on the table, the examination shifts to integration, deciding what will truthfully be implemented, who owns it, and what will change as a result.

A consistent structure protects the room from conversations that drift or get dominated by one or two personalities. It keeps smart people from wasting their time. Mastermind groups simply operationalize this structure at a higher level, so the room performs at a high standard every session.

The Me Plus Ultra Principle: Structure That Serves the Room

A strong room is built for the members, not the facilitator. The structure exists to make contribution easier, thinking clearer, and progress faster. When the room is designed correctly, the facilitator doesn't carry it, the members do. Their experience, questions, networks, and insights become the engine that drives breakthroughs.

Structure removes hiding places. If preparation is required, people prepare. If context is expected, vague thinking disappears. If clarifying questions are standard, the truth shows up fast. If integration is part of the process, execution becomes unavoidable. Members operate at a higher level because the environment is built for serious outcomes.

Mastermind groups (at least the ones designed correctly) represent the strongest form of this idea. They take the mechanics of a great room and build them into a system that produces consistent results.

Once you've been in a room built this way, the difference is immediate. Your thinking sharpens. Decisions get clearer because fewer things are left vague. Confidence grows, not from hype, but from knowing you're operating in an environment that forces better judgment. At that point, going back to looser, lower-standard rooms doesn't feel neutral. It feels like regression.

How Better Rooms Expand What You're Able to Think Through

06

At a certain level of success, leaders don't become risk-averse. They just stop noticing where their comfort zone has quietly moved. The things that once felt like real decisions start to feel routine. The moves that once required conviction now feel reasonable. Not because the leader changed, but because success resets what "normal" feels like. When you hit your goals or blow past them, the behaviors that got you there start to feel like the right default instead of something that should still be questioned.

That new comfort zone is hard to spot because nothing is obviously wrong. The business keeps running. People are doing their jobs. Decisions are still getting made. From the outside, everything looks good enough that there's no reason to slow down and challenge how things are working. When nothing forces that pause, standards don't rise, they just stagnate.

Over time, that has an effect on how leaders think. Decisions don't get worse, but they take longer. Conversations feel thoughtful, but they don't always land anywhere. You revisit topics instead of closing them. You leave meetings aligned in theory, but unclear on who's moving what forward. It all feels responsible, which makes it easy to miss the cost.

Experience plays a role here too. When you've been around long enough, you recognize patterns quickly. Sometimes too quickly. Ideas don't get shut down because they're bad, they get set aside because they sound familiar. You've heard it before. You've seen a version of it already. At some point, hearing something new starts to feel unlikely, so you stop expecting it.

This isn't arrogance; it's efficiency showing up in a different form. When there's no pressure around your thinking, efficiency starts shaping how decisions get made. If no one pushes on assumptions early, they don't get tested, they slowly settle in and become the plan. When timing goes unchallenged, decisions stretch out until they're no longer decisions at all, just the path of least resistance.

That's how friction builds without setting off alarms. Things don't break, they just get heavier. Growth doesn't stop, but it starts costing more time and energy than it should because everything still "works." Most leaders don't recognize what's happening until progress feels slower than it has any right to be.

How Smart Thinking Starts Keeping Decisions Open

At higher levels, leaders don't struggle because they lack intelligence. They struggle because the same thinking that once helped them navigate uncertainty starts protecting them from committing too early, too visibly, or too decisively. The thinking doesn't degrade, but it does become safer, and that shift is hard to notice while it's happening.

Smart leaders are wired to be thoughtful. They slow things down, consider tradeoffs, and look for second- and third-order consequences because those instincts have served them well. The problem shows up when there's no environment forcing clarity, because those same instincts stop improving decisions and start keeping them open. The analysis feels careful, the conversation sounds mature, and because nothing is obviously wrong, the cost stays hidden for longer than it should.

That's paralysis by analysis, not confusion or lack of intelligence, but the ability to keep a decision open by making the conversation smarter every time it comes up.

Isolation amplifies the problem because, on your own, there's no real cost to reopening the same decision again. No one challenges whether the additional thinking is actually improving the outcome or just delaying accountability, and over time the organization adapts to the pace the leader sets until hesitation starts to feel normal.

What Makes Delay Dangerous Isn't How It Feels

What makes delay dangerous isn't how it feels in the moment. It's that the consequences arrive later, disconnected from the decision that caused them.

The first cost shows up in timing. Opportunities don't usually disappear because someone else executed better; they disappear because the window quietly closed while a decision stayed open. The market moved or client expectations shifted. The moment passed without resistance because nothing felt urgent while it was happening.

Talent erosion follows. High-caliber people don't leave because of one bad call. They leave when direction never quite lands. When decisions stay provisional, strong operators stop committing their best energy to outcomes that may never materialize. They disengage, or they move toward environments where momentum is real and decisions actually close.

Strategy begins to drift the same way. Priorities blur when nothing hardens into commitment. Initiatives stack without resolution. Teams stay busy, but the business slowly loses coherence. Not because leadership lacks vision, but because vision never gets translated into decisions the organization can fully align behind.

There's also a cost leaders rarely name: Fatigue. Carrying open decisions is mentally expensive. When nothing closes, everything stays active. Conversations get revisited, timing gets questioned, and tension that should have been resolved keeps leaking into the next decision. Over time, that wears down decisiveness. The instinct to act gets replaced by the instinct to wait.

Eventually, hesitation becomes cultural. Teams learn that decisions are flexible instead of final. Accountability softens, urgency fades, and people adapt by protecting optionality instead of committing fully. What started as smart thinking turns into an organization that hesitates by default.

The danger isn't a single bad decision. It's the accumulation of decisions that never quite get made, and the quiet costs that stack up while leadership believes it's still being careful.

How Delay Becomes the Most Expensive Decision

Time doesn't respond to intent, it responds to structure. Once pressure fades from an environment, time stops working as a multiplier and starts working as a tax. It doesn't show up all at once or in dramatic ways. It shows up gradually, which is why almost everyone underestimates it.

The most dangerous part is the lag between cause and effect.. What happens today doesn't show up in results until much later, which makes it easy to misread progress. You're still working hard and the business is still moving, which is exactly why this goes unnoticed for as long as it does. The gap between input and return widens slowly, and because it widens quietly, it rarely triggers a course correction early enough to matter.

Over time, those delays begin stacking on top of each other in ways that are hard to reverse. Feedback arrives after it's useful. Corrections get applied later than they should, when the cost of change is higher and the margin for error is thinner. Nothing feels urgent in the moment, but over time, everything gets heavier to move.

Compression works the opposite way. When pressure is applied early, time collapses distance. Learning curves shorten. Mistakes surface while they're still cheap. Adjustments happen before habits harden. The same calendar produces very different outcomes depending on whether pressure shows up before or after momentum has already slowed.

What catches most leaders off guard isn't the slowdown itself. It's the moment when results finally reflect what's been happening beneath the surface for much longer than anyone wants to admit. By then, the patterns are already set, and reversing course is possible, but it's slower, more expensive, and far less forgiving than it would have been earlier.

How Pressure Changes What Decisions Feel Possible

What essentially changes in better rooms isn't confidence or personality. People don't walk out suddenly braver than they were before. What changes is the pressure around how decisions get made. The room shifts what feels normal, and once that happens, certain choices stop feeling as risky as they used to.

When you're surrounded by people who operate at a higher standard, you start feeling that standard before anyone ever points it out. You notice what gets questioned. You notice what doesn't get a pass. You notice how quickly vague thinking gets pushed into something more concrete. Nobody's trying to motivate anyone. What is expected just becomes clear.

The courage isn't internal; it shows up because the room makes hesitation harder to hide. It isn't from flipping on some internal switch. It's borrowed from the room. In those environments, clarity is treated as the baseline, follow-through is assumed rather than celebrated, and people remember what you said you'd do the last time you were in the room. That combination changes how decisions feel before you ever make them.

Over time, behavior adjusts without anyone needing to manage it. Leaders start asking better questions earlier, not because they're trying to improve themselves, but because that's how the room operates. Assumptions surface faster. Tradeoffs get named sooner. Things don't drag the way they do elsewhere, and no one has to explain why.

Once you've worked inside that kind of environment, it changes how everything else feels. Thinking alone isn't wrong, but it's slower, because there's nothing closing the loop between ideas and action. The contrast isn't emotional or motivational, it's structural.

In stronger rooms, standards are reinforced quietly through what gets questioned, what gets followed up on, and what's no longer tolerated. Over time, that shifts what feels normal, once that baseline expands, it becomes the floor you operate from.

What Better Rooms Do to Your Identity

07

There's a version of you that your old environment was perfectly designed to keep in place. Not because it wanted to hold you back, but because it needed you to be consistent, predictable, and reliable. The role you played mattered, and you played it well. Over time, that role hardened into your identity. You didn't just operate a certain way. You became that way.

The problem is that environments don't evolve at the same pace people do. They reward what works now, not what will be required next. When you stay in one long enough, it quietly trains you to optimize for fit instead of growth. You get better at meeting expectations that no longer stretch you. You refine behaviors that keep things running smoothly, and because everything still functions, it's easy to mistake stability for progress.

This is why identity is so difficult to examine honestly. It doesn't feel limiting; it feels earned. You've been useful, you've been respected, and you've carried responsibility when it mattered. Questioning that version of yourself doesn't feel like ambition. It feels unnecessary, even disloyal. The environment hasn't asked you to change, so why would you?

What you don't see yet is that the same environment that once amplified your strengths is now quietly protecting you from your next level. Not by holding you back, but by continuing to reward what it was built to reward.

When the Leader You've Been Stops Working

The hardest identity to let go of is the one that still works.

Not the one that failed or broke something, but the one that delivered results, earned trust, and kept people aligned. That identity doesn't feel outdated. It feels proven. And because it's proven, leaders defend it long after it stops being sufficient.

This is where most leadership conversations get it wrong. Resistance here isn't denial or ego; it's loyalty. Loyalty to instincts that protected the business. Loyalty to patterns that made things move. Loyalty to a way of showing up that once mattered deeply. Letting go of that identity doesn't feel like growth. It feels like abandoning something that still deserves respect.

I see this most often in leaders who built their authority by being decisive early, stepping in when things broke, and moving faster than everyone else in the room. That approach didn't just work, it became the reason people trusted them.

That loyalty creates a quiet bind. As long as that identity remains intact, authority feels secure. Decisions still feel familiar, confidence stays intact, and letting that version of yourself go doesn't come with a replacement waiting on the other side. It creates a gap where certainty used to be, and most leaders are conditioned to avoid that gap at all costs.

This is why people don't get pushed out of demanding settings. They step away instead. They don't frame it as fear or avoidance, but as timing, priorities or alignment. On paper, those explanations make sense. Underneath them is a simpler truth; staying would require operating without the identity that used to anchor them.

Nothing forces the decision out loud. There's no confrontation or rejection. Influence just becomes less automatic. Deference is no longer assumed. The role you occupied quietly dissolves, and you're left with a choice most people never name: protect who you've been, or question it without knowing what replaces it yet.

How Proximity Forces an Identity Shift

Up to this point, the focus has been on what rooms do. What matters here is what starts happening to you once you're inside them and staying there. The shift isn't announced. It shows up in the small ways your usual approach stops carrying the same weight it once did.

I didn't change how I showed up because I decided to. I changed because certain things stopped working the moment I was in closer proximity to people who operated differently. Questions didn't move as fast, assumptions didn't slide through, and explanations that used to be enough suddenly weren't. Nothing was hostile. Nothing was said out loud. The response just wasn't there.

That lack of response exposes what you've been relying on without calling it out. In familiar settings, confidence carries a lot of weight. People fill in gaps for you. In closer proximity to sharper operators, that buffer disappears. You're still heard, but ideas don't move forward until they're clear. Experience doesn't end discussion. It earns scrutiny.

What caught me off guard wasn't disagreement. It was how deliberate everyone was. People slowed things down without apologizing for it. Over time, that changes how you prepare. Not out of fear, but because you don't want to be sloppy in a place that isn't.

That's where identity starts to shift. Not because you're trying to reinvent yourself, but because you stop leaning on shortcuts that used to carry you. You notice when you're speaking from habit instead of clarity and start to feel the difference between being confident and being precise. Those moments add up.

Proximity works because it's consistent. One conversation doesn't change anything. But repeated exposure recalibrates your internal standard. You stop measuring yourself against what you used to get away with and start measuring yourself against what in fact holds up to the standards of the room.

At some point, you realize the shift has already happened. You're listening differently. You're speaking less, but with more intent. Contribution replaces control. Without anyone saying it explicitly, the identity you've been operating from starts to feel outdated, not because it was wrong, but because it's no longer enough.

The Identity Cost You Don't See Until It's Too Late

There's a point where identity stagnation stops being theoretical and starts becoming visible, even if no one names it. You're still present, still respected, still involved, but the center of gravity has shifted. The work moves forward without needing to pass through you in the same way, and no one explains why because nothing has technically gone wrong.

This is where accomplished leaders misread what's happening. They assume relevance fades only when performance drops or effort declines. In reality, relevance erodes when the environment no longer needs to bend around how you operate. Standards hold. Pace holds. Expectations stay fixed. What changes is how often your presence is required to move things forward.

You're not excluded. You're simply no longer central.

That shift doesn't feel like rejection. It feels like maturity. Like trust. Like the organization has finally learned to run without friction, that's exactly why it's dangerous. Because what's actually happening is quieter: influence is being redistributed, not removed, and you're learning about it after the fact.

Nothing announces the transition. You're still invited. Still heard. Still valued. You're just no longer shaping the hardest work by default.

That's the moment most people miss.

The Cost You Actually Pay

The real cost doesn't show up in how others treat you. It shows up in how you start making decisions once the environment stops pressing you the way it used to.

You begin choosing situations that feel cleaner, faster, and easier to control. Not because you've lost ambition, but because friction no longer feels like a signal worth listening to. Work that once sharpened you now registers as unnecessary drag, and challenges that used to energize you start to feel inefficient. The edge dulls quietly, not from lack of ability, but from lack of resistance.

Over time, preparation shifts without you noticing. You stop getting ready for scrutiny and start getting ready for alignment. Momentum begins to matter more than accuracy, and while decisions feel smoother, they stop demanding the kind of thinking that once distinguished you.

Experience starts carrying more weight than precision, and judgment replaces proof more often than it should. Nothing breaks, which is exactly why it's dangerous, but fewer things actually improve. You remain capable and confident, yet noticeably less exact than you used to be.

What you lose first isn't opportunity. It's calibration.

Without steady exposure to people who won't let things slide, your sense of what "good enough" looks like begins to drift. You start relying more on what has worked before than on what still holds up under pressure, and progress quietly shifts from expansive to incremental.

Eventually, that shows up in optionality. Not because doors close, but because the rooms that demand the most from you stop feeling worth the cost. Re-entry starts requiring adjustments you haven't practiced in a while, and the version of yourself you protected begins creating friction instead of leverage.

You don't lose status in the process, which is why it's so easy to miss what's happening. What you lose is the edge.

By the time you notice, you've been paying that price for longer than you realize.

Why High-Standard Settings Don't Let You Stay the Same

High standards don't organize themselves around individual comfort or identity. They organize around the integrity of the work and the shared outcomes that need to be produced. That purpose is established before anyone shows up and continues long after anyone leaves. Decisions still need to be made. Clarity still has to be reached. Momentum still has to be preserved. When that's true, a room like this cannot reorganize itself around individual preference without undermining what it exists to do.

That's why standards at this level don't need to be explained or enforced. They're already there. Expectations don't adjust based on who someone used to be or what they've accomplished before. Not because people don't matter, but because consistency is what makes the whole thing work. Once standards start bending for individuals, the system loses the very thing people came for in the first place.

A better comparison is professional sports. The league doesn't change the rules to accommodate veteran players who've been successful for a long time. The pace of the game stays the same. The expectations stay the same. If a player can still perform at that level, they stay relevant. If they can't, the game doesn't slow down for them. That isn't disrespect. It's how the integrity of the league is protected. The rules exist so the game works for everyone who's still in it.

The dynamic works the same way in high standard settings. Pace isn't an outcome anyone hopes for; it's a constraint that gets protected. Slowing things down to accommodate individual habits or styles erodes trust and lowers quality. Once that happens, the environment stops serving the people who were drawn to its standard in the first place.

This is why the group doesn't require explanation. Explanation invites negotiation, and negotiation invites exception. At this level, both are avoided by staying consistent. The bar isn't announced or justified. It simply stays where it is.

The standard doesn't push anyone out. It doesn't need to. It cannot carry static identities forward without weakening itself, and it will always protect its integrity in service of the people who rely on it.

Why Familiar Patterns Eventually Stop Holding

When leaders step away at this stage, they aren't leaving people or opportunity. They're stepping away from a standard that no longer adjusts to them. That distinction is what allows the decision to feel responsible instead of regressive. Nothing has failed. Nothing is broken. The only thing that's changed is that the work stopped bending.

What follows is rarely framed as retreating. It's framed as alignment. Leaders tell themselves things like:

"I'm choosing the setting where I create the most value."
"This is where my experience counts."
"I move faster here. My judgment matters more."

On their own, those statements sound reasonable. They're often true. The problem isn't the logic. It's what that logic quietly authorizes.

This is how disengagement becomes rational. Decisions that once required justification stop getting questioned, pushback starts to feel inefficient, and standards that demand more preparation or exposure begin to feel excessive rather than essential.

That's the loop. Capability starts to justify comfort, comfort gets reframed as clarity, and clarity becomes the reason you don't need anything more demanding. At no point does it feel like you've chosen the easier path. It feels like you've chosen the right one.

The cost shows up later, when efficiency starts limiting what's possible. By then, the story has hardened. You didn't leave because the standard was too high. You left because you believed you had nothing left to prove there.

How the Standard Rewrites the Leader

At this point, becoming a different kind of leader isn't about ambition. It's about alignment. The standard is already set, and it isn't waiting to be negotiated. What changes is how you operate in relation to it.

Authority gets earned differently at this level. Experience might get you heard, but it doesn't move the work forward on its own. What matters is how clearly you frame problems, how cleanly you define decisions, and whether people trust you to follow through.

Preparation shifts along with it. You spend more time thinking about the question than rehearsing the answer. You show up expecting friction instead of validation, and you stop measuring success by being right. Being useful starts to matter more.

Over time, your language becomes precise and the unnecessary explanation falls away. Decisions feel cleaner because you've learned when to push and when to stay open. None of this is taught directly. It's learned through exposure, through consequence, and through a standard that doesn't move to accommodate you.

Leadership stops being about holding position and starts being about holding the line. Responsibility isn't assigned. It's assumed.

How Members Transform Each Other Through the Standard

What makes this work inside Me Plus Ultra is the caliber of the people who show up and the way they hold each other to a shared standard. The working session doesn't create that discipline. It gives it somewhere to compound. The value comes from members who are willing to challenge each other honestly and stay with the issue long enough for something real to change.

Over time, members become more deliberate about what they bring forward and more precise about how they frame it. Loose thinking and overconfidence don't last long, because the standard doesn't reward either.

Authority comes from contribution. Experience still matters, but only when it sharpens the work instead of shortcutting it. Everyone is exposed to the same expectations, and that shared exposure changes how members see themselves.

As this repeats, identity shifts become apparent without being named. Members ask better questions. They take more time with decisions that matter. They pressure-test their own instincts before relying on them. Preparation improves and follow-through streamlines, not because anyone announces it, but because it's learned over time.

Eventually, the influence of the group extends beyond the session itself. Members carry the standard into meetings, decisions, and conversations elsewhere. They become harder to rush, harder to impress, and harder to pull into shallow agreement.

That's how transformation happens inside Me Plus Ultra. Not through inspiration, and not because of any single voice. It happens because capable people commit to holding the same line together, year after year. The identity shift isn't announced. It's practiced, and the standard that makes it possible doesn't belong to the brand. It belongs to the members who carry it forward.

The Mechanics of High-Performance Rooms

08

Momentum doesn't slow because people forget how to work. It slows when conversations are allowed to end without finishing what they started.

When that happens, the work doesn't disappear. It gets pushed somewhere else. It shows up later as coordination, follow-up, reminders, and extra effort applied outside the room. That's usually when leaders feel the drag, long after the moment where it more accurately began.

High-performance rooms are built around a simple requirement: important work has to be completed while everyone who matters is still present. That changes what a conversation is allowed to be. Clarity isn't optional. Responsibility doesn't get implied. What happens next isn't left for later. The room either produces something that can carry forward on its own, or it hasn't done its job yet.

That's the first mechanic at work. Work finishes where it starts, or it never in reality finishes.

How to Tell Whether or Not a Room Actually Worked

If you want to know whether a room did its job, don't judge it by how engaged the conversation felt while you were in it. Pay attention to what follows you home.

In a strong room, decisions leave with you. Not as loose intentions or provisional agreements, but as conclusions that hold their shape once the conversation ends. You know what moved, what didn't, and why. The question that brought you into the room doesn't stay open in the background, quietly competing for attention the rest of the week. It's either resolved or clearly owned, with next steps that don't require reinterpretation.

Just as important, certain things stop being debated. Issues that have already been pressure-tested don't resurface in slightly different forms. You don't find yourself re-explaining the same context to different people or reopening conversations to defend a decision that was supposedly made. The work doesn't trail behind you asking for clarification, alignment, or reassurance. It's finished enough to stand on its own.

What usually feels lighter isn't the workload, it's the mental overhead. You're not carrying unresolved tension from the room into unrelated decisions. You're not replaying exchanges in your head to see if you missed something or wondering whether the group actually agreed or just ran out of time. The clarity created in the room frees up attention instead of consuming it.

Weak rooms leave a different residue. Decisions feel technically made but practically unfinished. Conversations echo back through follow-ups, side discussions, and second guesses. Issues you thought were settled quietly reappear, often framed as new concerns, even though they're the same unresolved ones. Nothing feels urgent enough to force closure, so everything stays partially active.

That's the real test. Strong rooms reduce what follows you home. Weak rooms multiply it.

You don't need to analyze the personalities, the facilitation style, or how smart the conversation sounded. Just notice whether the room simplified your world afterward or made it heavier. High-performance rooms earn their value by how little unfinished work they leave behind.

Clarity Cannot Exist Without Forced Issue Definition

Clarity doesn't come from talking longer or adding more context. It comes from identifying the actual issue that needs a decision attached to it.

Without that constraint, conversations gravitate toward what's easiest to discuss. The conversation fills with context, side issues, and commentary that all sound relevant, but none of it forces the decision into the open. The room stays active without getting sharper.

Imagine a leader bringing a concern about growth slowing. The conversation immediately fills with discussion about marketing spend, sales performance, team capacity, and market conditions. All of those things matter, but none of them are yet the issue. Until the room forces the question, *what specific decision needs to be made right now,* the discussion keeps going in circles without anywhere execution can actually take hold.

Once the real issue is revealed, the dynamic changes. The conversation finally has a center. Pressure lands where it belongs, and everything else either supports that decision or falls away. The room doesn't need momentum or facilitation at that point because it knows exactly what it's there to resolve.

That's the mechanic here. Clarity has to be required before anything else can move.

Decisions Don't Close Without Structural Pressure

Decisions don't close because everyone nods. They close because the conversation reaches a point where ambiguity isn't allowed to linger.

Without that pressure, decisions stay reversible. People move on, but the decision itself never fully settles. It can still be reinterpreted or postponed once it leaves the room, which shows up later as hesitation during execution.

Think about golf. Standing over a putt, you can read the green, adjust your stance, take practice strokes, and feel confident about the line. But nothing happens until you commit and hit the ball. Until that moment, everything is still theoretical. The pressure isn't emotional, it's structural. The game forces a moment where you either take the shot or you don't.

Decisions work the same way in a room. Until the structure forces commitment, the decision is just preparation. Where that uncertainty gets resolved matters. Either it's handled while the people who own the decision are still present, or it gets pushed downstream into execution where it's harder to see and more expensive to deal with.

That pressure doesn't come from urgency or authority. It comes from how the conversation is allowed to end. When the room requires decisions to harden before moving on, ambiguity has nowhere to hide. That's the mechanic at work here. A decision isn't finished until uncertainty is resolved while everyone is still in the room.

Progress Stalls When Ownership Is Implicit

A conversation can feel clear and still fail to move anything forward. The direction sounds right. The next steps seem obvious. But once people leave, the actions don't belong to anyone in particular.

That gap usually shows up when responsibility is assumed instead of settled. The group leaves believing alignment happened, but alignment without ownership doesn't carry very far on its own.

Anyone who has planned a real event has seen this play out. The group aligns on the experience, the timing, and the goals. Everything feels clear in the room. Then deadlines start approaching and the gaps surface. People scramble to make up ground. Conversations pick back up. Extra effort gets applied. Things eventually come together, but only because pressure arrives from the outside.

The issue was never commitment. Responsibility just wasn't resolved while everyone was still in the room. When ownership is settled before the conversation ends, execution stops relying on urgency to correct what structure should have handled earlier. The mechanic requires responsibility to be explicitly resolved inside the conversation, not recovered later.

External Expertise Only Works After Internal Clarity

Outside perspective can be useful, but it only helps after a room has done the harder work of deciding what actually needs to be decided. Most failures with consultants, advisors, or outside experts don't come from bad advice. They come from inviting insight into a conversation that hasn't yet earned it.

This usually happens when a group senses something isn't working and jumps straight to looking outward for answers. The room fills with experience, examples, and recommendations pulled from other companies or other situations. Everyone feels engaged and the conversation has energy, but once people leave, nothing changes in a way that holds. The advice doesn't get rejected. It just floats, because there was never a clear decision for it to attach to.

What the room was missing wasn't intelligence or perspective. It was clarity about what problem actually mattered enough to force a call.

Without that clarity, expertise spreads the conversation wider instead of pulling it tighter. Each suggestion opens another possible direction. The group ends up comparing ideas rather than choosing between them, which feels productive in the moment but creates hesitation once execution begins. The advice wasn't wrong. It simply arrived before the room had given it a place to land.

When the issue is clearly defined first, the effect of outside perspective changes completely. Advice stops being theoretical and starts becoming directional because it's reacting to a specific decision that needs to be made. Experience gets filtered instead of piled on. Disagreement becomes useful- not because people are more aligned- but because they're arguing within the same boundary instead of talking past each other.

The order is what matters. Expertise does not create clarity. Clarity creates the conditions where expertise can actually do its job. When that sequence is respected, insight compresses decisions instead of complicating them, and progress comes from choosing rather than continuing to discuss.

Structured Accountability Without Bureaucracy

In lower standard rooms, accountability usually unravels after the conversation ends.

When commitments aren't settled before people move on, progress starts depending on a series of reminders, check-ins, and follow-up outside the room. The work still advances, but only because someone keeps actively pushing it forward.

In rooms where accountability is structural, commitments don't dissolve between sessions. Responsibility is clear, progress is visible, and the next conversation builds on the last one instead of restarting it. The work carries forward without needing to be chased.

The final mechanic is that accountability is established in the room, not managed afterward.

How the Mechanics Hold in the Real World

The reason Me Plus Ultra exists has less to do with insight and more to do with what happens after insight is shared. Over time, through the wrong rooms, wasted conferences, and admittedly, even the earliest versions of Business Bourbon & Cigars, it became clear that strong conversations weren't the issue. What failed was what happened once people returned to their businesses.

Decisions that felt settled during discussion quietly reopened later. Ownership blurred once teams, calendars, and real constraints entered the picture. Energy faded because nothing in the environment protected the decisions after the room cleared. That pattern wasn't occasional. It was consistent.

What followed wasn't an attempt to improve discussion quality or create better experiences. It was a decision to design rooms that behaved differently once pressure showed up. The mechanics you've read about earlier in this chapter weren't built as theory. They were shaped by where work repeatedly broke down when reality took over.

Before the Spotlight Ever Turns On

One of the most important differences in how Me Plus Ultra operates happens before an issue ever reaches the group's shared time. Allowing surface-level problems into the room slowed everything else down because they invited commentary instead of decisions and absorbed energy without changing outcomes.

That led to a higher standard for what earned the room's attention. Issues needed to arrive defined enough to support a real decision, not just a productive conversation. This wasn't about control. It was about respecting the experience in the room and refusing to spend it discovering problems that hadn't been thought through yet.

Before a member ever steps into the spotlight, the issue they think they have is pressed down. Assumptions surface and the framing narrows. In many cases, the question itself changes once it's forced to stand on its own without explanation filling in the gaps. What moves it forward isn't polish. It's that the issue can survive scrutiny without expanding.

That pre-work doesn't stay private. The issue, its current framing, and the paths that have already been ruled out are shared ahead of time. Members arrive clear and focused rather than simply informed. Clarifying questions start sharper because the groundwork has already been laid. By the time the session begins, the issue is narrow enough to test, real enough to challenge, and specific enough to support a decision.

Inside the Virtual Sessions

When the virtual sessions begin, the room doesn't rush toward solutions. The first job is to determine whether the issue in front of the room can undeniably support a decision that changes what happens next. The conversation stays there, asking sharper and sharper questions, until the real problem is clear enough that a decision can take hold once the session ends.

Take a problem almost every growing company runs into: new sales reps aren't getting productive fast enough.

That's how it's usually brought into a room. It sounds practical. It feels urgent. In most environments, that's enough to trigger ideas like better onboarding, more training, new scripts, different incentives, stronger managers. The conversation is filled with options, but no decision has appeared yet.

In this room, that framing doesn't move the conversation forward. The pace slows and the issue locks in. Someone asks how long it genuinely takes a new rep to close their first deal. Another asks where deals stall most often in the first ninety days. Another question surfaces about what happens if nothing changes and churn stays where it is.

That pressure changes the problem. What started as "ramp-up time" becomes a concrete decision. Leadership may allow pricing flexibility early so reps gain confidence with early wins. Certain accounts may stop being withheld too long. The organization may accept short-term margin pressure to avoid long-term attrition.

If a decision gets made, behavior changes immediately. Reps close deals sooner, confidence builds naturally, and attrition drops because early success changes how long people stay in the game. If no decision gets made, none of the advice matters, because the constraint never moves.

That's the difference between a topic that generates conversation and an issue that can carry weight once it leaves the room.

Up to this point, you've seen how these mechanics operate in recurring, virtual settings. What changes next isn't the standard, it's the intensity.

Why the Same Mechanics Show Up Differently at Business Bourbon & Cigars

The mastermind sessions at our flagship Business Bourbon & Cigars leadership retreat exist to test whether these mechanics still hold true when the problems are fully real and the pressure is immediate. Each session is built around a leader bringing a real-life situation from their business, something active, unresolved, and already carrying consequences they'd rather not keep paying for. The room has a fixed amount of time to move from situation to decision without skipping the hard parts in between.

There isn't space to linger in diagnosis or explore ideas that can't survive execution. The issue has to be clarified quickly, the decision boundary has to be named, and ownership has to be resolved in a way that still makes sense once the leader leaves the table and returns to their organization. If the decision can't hold up outside the room, it isn't finished inside it.

What makes this work at scale is exposure to multiple real life situations under the same structural expectations. Each of our leadership retreats include several mastermind sessions, and attendees rotate tables between them. When a leader finishes a session, that work is complete. The next table brings an entirely different situation and a different mission. Over the course of a full event, members don't revisit the same problem repeatedly, **they experience how different problems behave when they're forced through the same mechanics.**

Patterns surface quickly. Participants recognize which issues sharpen under pressure and which ones expand. They see how ownership either survives the room or quietly dissolves when it isn't resolved early enough. In some cases, sessions build on each other, not because the same problem is being reworked, but because relevant insight learned in one situation sharpens how another one is approached.

The workbook provided to every participant isn't there to teach anyone how to think. It exists to prevent gaps. It forces the issue, the decision, ownership, and contingencies to stay intact as the work moves forward. By the time a session ends, the problem is carried far enough that execution of the solution doesn't depend on interpretation or follow-up explanation.

The mechanics don't change from the virtual sessions. The environment does. Time is tighter. Pressure is immediate. Exposure is higher. What survives that setting tends to survive once the leader goes back to the business because it has already been tested under real pressure.

What Happens After the Session Ends

In Me Plus Ultra, decisions don't disappear once the session ends. What gets decided in the room is carried forward into execution quickly enough that reality either confirms it or breaks it. Members document the real issue they committed to solving and what they are responsible for owning as execution begins.

That visibility prevents reinterpretation. Optimism gets checked early. Ownership becomes harder to soften once real constraints appear. Other members can see the progress, add perspective, and surface risks before they become expensive surprises.

When the group comes back together, the conversation doesn't begin with lukewarm summaries of what was supposed to happen. Everyone already knows what was supposed to happen. If it didn't, the focus isn't on effort or intention. It goes back to the mechanics that failed to hold once pressure showed up and addresses them directly.

That's how accountability exists without bureaucracy. The work stays exposed just long enough to either hold up in execution or reveal what still isn't true.

Why These Rooms Change How Relationships Form

By now, the mechanics should be familiar. Issues are clearly defined before they enter the room. Decisions are forced to close. Ownership survives beyond the conversation. What's easy to miss is what those mechanics do to the people inside the room once they're repeated over time.

In most environments, relationships form slowly because trust is built on surface signals like titles, confidence, or proximity. Networking feels awkward because no one knows what they can safely ask for or offer without overstepping. Conversations stay polite, and value remains vague.

These rooms behave differently because contribution comes first.

When members consistently pressure-test each other's decisions, challenge assumptions, and help carry real problems forward, posturing stops working. Credibility isn't claimed. It's observed through preparation, clarity, and follow-through. Over time, people stop guarding ideas because everyone can see what holds up and what doesn't.

At Business Bourbon & Cigars, relationships don't form through mingling or shared interests. They form because the structure puts people to work together immediately. Each mastermind session places leaders at a different table, working on a different real situation pulled directly from someone's business. In one session, you're helping a founder untangle a hiring decision. In the next, you're pressure-testing a growth constraint or a leadership bottleneck. You're not introducing yourself, you're contributing.

By the time the tables rotate again, you've already seen how someone thinks, where their experience is real, and how they show up under pressure. That repeats across multiple sessions with different people and different problems. Even leaders who normally struggle with networking find themselves forming strong connections because the work does the social lifting for them. When the event ends, follow-up doesn't feel forced. It feels natural because trust wasn't built through conversation, it was built through shared problem-solving, repeated in real time.

That's why rooms like this are sometimes hard to explain until you experience them. On the surface, they don't look dramatic because there's nothing being performed and nothing being propped up with forced hype or forced energy. What people feel instead is the weight of real work being carried out together and the quiet confidence that comes from knowing it will hold up once everyone leaves. That's usually the moment leaders realize they've been trying to describe something that can't be explained, it has to be experienced.

What High-Standard Rooms Require From You

09

Up to this point, the focus has been on what high-standard rooms do. Now we're going to dive into what they require, and the shift matters because the burden changes before most people realize it has.

In high-standard rooms, what you've done before doesn't create momentum on its own. Experience may earn access, but it doesn't guarantee forward progress. What determines whether the room engages is whether your thinking is clear enough *right now* to be examined, challenged, and finished without relying on further explanation after the fact. Past results don't get argued with, but they also don't carry present work.

That's where the line moves. In these rooms, showing up with a loosely defined issue and expecting the group to help you solve it doesn't work anymore. Relying on past wins, reputation, or experience to carry a half-formed thought doesn't work either. The room engages when you've already done the work to define the problem, explain why it matters now, and bring something concrete to the table. Preparation, clarity, and follow-through aren't assumed; they're evident. Nothing about that shift gets announced or explained. The room simply responds to how you show up and what you bring.

What the Room Requires Before It Engages with You

Preparation isn't about merely doing your homework; it's how the room decides whether to engage with you at all. That doesn't mean having your slides, notes, or story polished. It means arriving already clear on what decision you're trying to make or what problem you're asking the room to help solve. The room isn't there to help you think out loud until something useful appears. It's there to pressure-test thinking that's already formed enough to start from.

The difference shows up immediately. Someone who's prepared can state the issue clearly, explain why it matters now, and outline what they've already considered. They don't ramble on or search for the point while others wait. The room can engage because there's something solid to push against. When that foundation isn't there, the conversation stalls, not because people aren't willing to help, but because the room is forced to spend its time figuring out what the real problem is instead of helping solve it. That's also why, in rooms that take the work seriously, people don't step into the spotlight cold. The thinking firms up before the room ever engages.

This is where many leaders misunderstand what preparation means. They assume it's about having answers. It isn't. It's about having done enough thinking to know where the uncertainty really lives. A prepared leader can say, "Here's the decision I'm stuck on," or "Here's the constraint I can't get past," without drifting into background, history, or justification. That clarity is what allows the room to work the decision instead of working through explanations.

Preparation also signals respect, not in a performative way, but in a practical one. You're asking other experienced leaders to give you their time, attention, and judgment. The expectation is that you've already taken the issue as far as you reasonably can on your own. The room isn't there to replace that effort. It's there to sharpen it.

When preparation is missing, the room doesn't call it out directly. It doesn't need to. Questions get slower, engagement thins, and the energy shifts. Not as punishment, but as a natural response to unclear situations. Over time, that feedback becomes consistent enough that it's impossible to miss. The room moves fastest when the thinking is ready, and it waits when it isn't.

That's why preparation isn't optional or flexible. It's the condition that determines whether the room can materially help you or not, and once you see that pattern clearly, you start preparing differently. Not to impress anyone, but because it's the only way the work actually moves forward.

What Your Pattern of Showing Up Teaches the Room

Elite rooms don't reset every time you walk into them. They don't keep score in visible ways or announce conclusions, but they do learn. Over time, the room notices which conversations land and which ones drift, which issues close and which ones quietly linger. That accumulation shapes how the room listens well before any response is given.

This is where responsibility compounds. When a leader consistently brings challenges that resolve cleanly, the room responds differently. Questions get sharper. Pushback gets more direct. The room invests more pressure because it knows the effort will convert into movement. When a leader repeatedly brings problems that stay open, the response shifts in the opposite direction. Engagement becomes cautious, energy spreads thinner, and attention reallocates. Not out of frustration, but out of judgment about where effort in fact produces results.

Nothing about this process is personal. It's operational. Pressure gets allocated where it pays off. Clarity that should already exist doesn't get chased, and work that hasn't shown it will land doesn't keep getting pushed. Over time, that changes the experience of being in the room. Some people feel increasingly challenged. Others feel the room go quieter around them. In both cases, the standard hasn't moved; the response has.

This is the part most people never connect back to themselves. The shift gets interpreted as chemistry or fit when it's really feedback. The room is responding to a pattern of how you bring issues to the group, not to confidence, personality, or reputation. Attention follows finish. Pressure follows clarity. Silence follows work that can't carry itself beyond the room.

Unfinished work isn't punished, but it isn't forgotten either. Over time, how the room remembers you shapes how much it's willing to invest the next time you step forward.

When You're Ready for the Room That Changes Everything

10

Most people don't delay changing rooms because they lack ambition or capability. They delay because they're waiting for a feeling that never quite arrives. Readiness is something that gets treated like an internal milestone, that shows up once confidence is high enough, uncertainty is low enough, and the risk feels manageable.

That signal almost never appears. What shows up instead is hesitation dressed up as patience. Leaders tell themselves they just need a little more time, a little more understanding, or a few more wins before stepping into an elite environment.

No one enters fully ready. These rooms aren't designed to reward polish or finished answers. What matters is whether you're willing to operate at a higher standard while your thinking is still being sharpened.

This is where many strong leaders misread the moment. They assume readiness means fewer questions, more control, or tighter answers. In practice, it shows up as willingness. Willingness to prepare differently. Willingness to let thinking be examined. Willingness to finish work in public instead of protecting it in private.

That decision changes how the room meets you. When you stop waiting to feel ready and start choosing to meet the standard, the room does what it's built to do. It applies pressure where it matters, removes ambiguity faster, and forces clarity sooner. Not because you're special, but because you've committed to how the work gets done.

From here on, the question isn't whether you're ready. It's whether you're willing to decide how you'll operate when the standard no longer adjusts to you.

What You Give Up When You Step Into a Higher-Standard Room

Stepping into a room like this doesn't simply demand more effort or preparation. It requires giving up advantages that have quietly made your current environments workable, which is why the decision carries more consequence than it first appears.

One of the first things that disappears is control over how your situation gets framed. You no longer decide which details matter most, how much context gets offered, or when the conversation moves forward. The room presses on what is structurally true rather than what is most comfortable to explain, and once that pressure is applied, the story sharpens whether you are ready for it or not.

Another shift shows up around status inside the conversation. In many rooms, experience creates deference and buys room to speak without resistance. In higher-standard rooms, that dynamic changes. Experience doesn't create insulation; it creates expectation. The more capable you are, the more directly your thinking is examined, because the room assumes you can withstand scrutiny without needing protection.

The ability to rely on competence as cover also fades quickly. Prior wins no longer compensate for unfinished thinking. Reputation doesn't soften vagueness. Intensity doesn't substitute for clarity. Ideas that haven't been pressure-tested don't get rescued by the group, and commitments that aren't grounded don't quietly pass. If something matters, the room expects it to close. If it doesn't, the lack of resolution becomes apparent without anyone needing to point it out.

Comfort erodes for similar reasons. The environment doesn't absorb hesitation or smooth over uncertainty. Silence doesn't shield you, and elegant language doesn't buy time. Questions surface what hasn't been decided instead of allowing it to sit unresolved. For leaders who are used to being the stabilizing force in every setting, that shift can feel disorienting at first.

None of this feels harsh or aggressive in practice. It feels clarifying. That clarity is exactly what makes the transition difficult, because clarity always removes something before it replaces it.

What Replaces It

What takes the place of control is a shared understanding of reality. You are no longer responsible for holding everything together on your own, because the room sees the problem alongside you rather than through you. Decisions stop depending on how well you reinforce them afterward, because they've already been worked to a point where they can carry forward without constant attention.

What replaces narrative dominance is a different form of respect. Credibility isn't assumed or claimed; it's earned through preparation, coherence, and follow-through. The respect that develops in these environments carries more weight precisely because it's grounded in how your thinking performs under pressure, not in how confidently it's presented.

Comfort gives way to compression. Time behaves differently when fewer things are left open. Decisions settle faster, not because people rush, but because ambiguity doesn't linger. The distance between insight and execution shortens, and conversations stop looping because the work has actually been finished instead of deferred.

What replaces the ability to hide is a relief of a different kind. It isn't relief from responsibility, but relief from carrying it alone. Pressure gets distributed among people who are capable of holding it. Thinking sharpens. The load lightens, not because expectations drop, but because they're finally shared at the level where they belong.

This is the threshold the chapter is pointing toward. The choice isn't about joining a better conversation or accessing sharper insight. It's about whether you are willing to release the protections that made lower-standard rooms feel manageable in exchange for an environment that no longer allows you to rely on them.

Leaving Comfort for Standards

Leaving comfort isn't about fixing something that's broken. It's about acknowledging a trade you're already making and deciding whether you're willing to keep paying for it.

By the time this choice becomes obvious, you already know what comfort gives you. You know how to meet expectations without redefining them. You know how to stay effective without being fully examined. You know how to operate in ways that protect momentum, reputation, and confidence at the same time. None of that is accidental. It's the result of learning exactly how much is required—and how much isn't.

Standards interrupt that arrangement. They don't allow you to manage perception or pace exposure. They don't flex around what you've already proven. The problem is either clear enough to discuss or it isn't. The decision is either made or it isn't. That shift is what makes the move costly. You're no longer insulated by what's familiar. You're measured by what holds up in real time.

This is where hesitation shows up, even for capable leaders. Not because they doubt their ability, but because they recognize what's being surrendered. Comfort allows you to stay effective without being fully exposed. Standards remove that option. They surface gaps sooner, force decisions faster, and reduce the margin for unfinished thinking.

The trade is simple, even if it's uncomfortable to admit. Comfort doesn't hold you steady; it slowly lowers the bar around you. What once required effort becomes routine. What once demanded clarity gets handled on instinct. Over time, you're not maintaining your level, you're quietly slipping below it while everything still feels familiar. Standards interrupt that slide. They force you to prove, again and again, that what you're doing still holds up. You don't leave comfort because it's wrong. You leave it because staying there eventually costs you ground you didn't realize you were losing, until that loss shows up as discomfort you can't ignore.

By the time someone chooses standards over comfort, the question has already shifted. They're no longer asking whether the room will challenge them. They're asking whether staying comfortable is quietly costing them more than they're willing to admit.

The Psychology of Crossing Thresholds

What destabilizes this moment isn't uncertainty about your mastery. It's that the signals you relied on no longer mean what they used to.

When you step into an elite room, familiar instincts stop working the way they used to. Effort no longer converts cleanly into momentum. Experience stops smoothing decisions. Confidence stops shortening the distance between discussion and action. Nothing is explicitly wrong, but your internal feedback loop goes quiet. The cues you've relied on for years don't register the same way, and for a stretch, it's hard to tell whether you're progressing or slipping.

This is where many people misread the moment. They interpret the uncertainty as a readiness issue, when in reality it's a calibration issue. Comfort was doing more guiding than they realized, and that guide has just been removed. The tension they feel isn't a warning. It's the psychological gap between operating standards, where old instincts lose authority and new ones haven't fully formed yet.

What changes first isn't how you behave, but how uncomfortable you feel inside your own thinking. Habits that once provided traction no longer give you certainty. Instincts that used to feel reliable start requiring explanation. You become more aware of where your thinking is thin, where you're buying time, and where you're hoping familiarity will carry you through.

That awareness is uncomfortable because it doesn't come with immediate replacement. You're not failing; you're operating without the shortcuts that previously protected you. Until new patterns form, everything feels slower, heavier, and more deliberate than you're used to.

Waiting doesn't stabilize this moment. Staying put doesn't make the signals clearer. The only way through a threshold is to operate at the new standard until it stops feeling new and starts feeling normal. Until then the discomfort remains, doing exactly what it's supposed to do, marking the space between levels.

That's why this transition feels exposing. The familiar protections are gone, and the new ones haven't formed yet. What's left is visibility, and once that's in play, there's no hiding behind comfort anymore.

Why Elite Rooms Don't Let You Hide

Elite rooms don't remove cover to increase accountability. They remove it because hiding changes how *you* participate long before it changes anything else.

When hiding is an option, it rarely feels like avoidance. It feels strategic. You listen carefully and contribute selectively. You stay close enough to the work to remain informed, but far enough away to avoid full exposure. Nothing about that feels wrong in the moment.

Over time, though, it changes how you show up. You're present, but not fully in it, and that distance quietly compounds. Eventually, participation stops being ambiguous. You're either willing to bring your thinking forward or you're not, and the difference becomes clear without anyone needing to say it out loud.

This is why elite rooms feel demanding in a way others don't. They don't let you manage proximity. You can't stay informed without being involved. You can't maintain influence without contributions that hold up under pressure. Participation stops being something you signal and becomes something you demonstrate repeatedly.

Over time, that exposure changes you. It removes the option to protect comfort while telling yourself you're still growing. You start to see where you hesitate, where you soften your position, and where you avoid finishing thoughts that might be challenged. None of that is meant to embarrass you. It's meant to make your patterns apparent to you.

That's the real reason elite rooms don't let you hide. Allowing cover doesn't protect you; it protects the habits that keep you operating below your capacity. By removing it, the room forces an honest relationship with how you show up, not once, but over time.

Becoming the Person Who Belongs in Better Rooms

Belonging in better rooms isn't something you earn once and carry with you. It's something that gets tested every time you walk in. The test shows up before outcomes exist, when the work is unfinished, responsibility is still exposed, and your thinking has to stand on its own. What matters in those moments isn't who you've been or what you've built, but how willing you are to risk your judgment publicly while the work is still taking shape.

People often assume belonging is granted by access. That once you're inside the room, the question is settled. In reality, access only removes the barrier to entry. What determines whether you belong is what happens after that, how prepared you are to finish what you start, and how willing you are to let your thinking be examined without protecting it.

Belonging reveals itself through behavior. Over time, patterns become obvious. Some people consistently contribute, add clarity, and help close decisions. Others relay information, echo what's already been said, or stay safely adjacent to the discussion without shaping it.

Becoming someone who belongs isn't about changing who you are. It's about deciding how you operate when the standard is excellence. It means preparing even when no one is checking. Being precise even when vagueness would pass. Finishing work in the room instead of exporting it downstream. These aren't traits, they're choices made repeatedly.

What separates people in elite environments isn't potential. It's consistency. Showing up the same way when the work is exposed, the outcome isn't guaranteed, and there's no room to hide behind effort alone. Over time, that consistency creates operational trust. The room invests where it knows effort will convert into progress.

There is no threshold you cross where belonging becomes permanent. There's only a standard you choose to meet, again and again. The room doesn't decide whether you belong. Your behavior does.

You're Already Choosing a Room

By the time you reach the end of this book, it should be clear that you're already operating inside an environment that shapes you in very real ways. Not as an idea or a metaphor, but through the standards it enforces, the expectations it tolerates, and the kind of work it allows to move forward. That environment may be one you chose deliberately, or one you stepped into years ago and never questioned. Either way, it has been training you quietly through what it requires and what it lets slide.

Most people assume choice only shows up when they actively decide to leave or change something. Until then, they treat staying as neutral, as if nothing meaningful is happening in the background. But staying is not neutral. It's an ongoing decision reinforced by habit, familiarity, and time. Even when nothing dramatic occurs, the environment continues to shape how you prepare, how clearly you think, and how much unfinished work becomes acceptable.

Over time, this shaping doesn't feel disruptive. It feels normal. You adjust your expectations to match the conditions around you. The questions you bring into conversations become more contained. The level of preparation you consider sufficient recalibrates. Not because you lost capability or ambition, but because the environment stopped insisting on more. The change is gradual enough that it rarely registers as a problem while it's happening.

This is where people get misled. From the inside, it feels like stability.

From the outside, it looks like stalled momentum. Because nothing breaks, nothing forces attention. You continue producing results, meeting expectations, and carrying responsibility competently enough that no immediate consequence appears. Growth doesn't stop in a way that's easy to detect. It thins out. The slope changes slightly, and unless you're paying close attention, it's easy to mistake continuity for progress.

Standards don't pause while this happens. They don't wait for timing or readiness. They continue to operate, whether you engage them directly or not. When you place yourself in environments that enforce clarity, preparation and completion. The pressure is immediate and unmistakable. When you don't, the cost shows up later- often in ways that are harder to trace back to a single decision. It shows up as longer cycles, slower resolution, and the sense that you're expending more effort for less movement than you did in the past.

The most deceptive part is that nothing feels urgent while this is unfolding. You're still functioning well enough to be trusted and relied upon, which is exactly why nothing forces the issue. That's what makes inertia dangerous for capable people. Competence absorbs friction. Experience smooths over inefficiencies. Results buy time. You can operate effectively inside an environment long after it has stopped challenging you in meaningful ways, and that effectiveness delays the moment when the cost becomes obvious.

There is no point at which staying becomes free. Every year spent in an environment that doesn't demand your best thinking is a year where that thinking isn't being sharpened. Every cycle without real pressure makes the next one harder to step into, not because you're less capable, but because you're less conditioned for it. Conditioning matters more than most people want to admit, especially at higher levels where raw effort is no longer the constraint.

This isn't an argument for constant movement or dissatisfaction. There are seasons where staying is the right decision. But staying should be deliberate, not accidental. It should be chosen with full awareness of what the environment is reinforcing and what it is allowing to fade. The difference between those two versions of staying is significant, even if it doesn't look dramatic on the surface.

People who choose their environments carefully understand something that often goes unspoken.

Growth isn't driven by motivation or intent. It's driven by repeated exposure to standards that don't negotiate.

When clarity, preparation, and follow-through are required consistently, they stop feeling exceptional and start feeling normal. When they aren't, those same qualities weaken over time, regardless of talent or experience.

By now, you've seen what better environments do to thinking, identity, and execution. You've seen how standards shape behavior long before outcomes are visible. None of that is theoretical. The only unresolved question is whether you're willing to acknowledge that choosing not to choose is still a choice, and that time will continue to make choices on your behalf if you don't interfere.

You are already choosing a room through what you tolerate, what you accept, and what you allow to become normal. That choice is being reinforced every week, in every meeting, and in every moment where preparation either happens fully or gets deferred. Whether you name it or not, the decision is in motion.

That's where this book ends. Not with an invitation or a prescription, but with a reality that's already underway. Your environment is shaping you now, and it will continue to do so until you decide otherwise.

Conclusion

This book wasn't written to convince you to make a change. It was written to help you see more clearly what is already shaping you.

By now, the pattern should be familiar. Rooms don't just host conversations. They influence what feels acceptable to leave unfinished, what questions get asked, and how much precision is required before a decision takes form. Over time, those standards become internalized as part of you. They stop feeling like external pressure and start feeling like "how things work."

That's why this dynamic is so easy to miss. Nothing announces itself as a problem. Progress continues because people remain capable, and yet, something subtle shifts. The environments you rely on begin reinforcing what you already know how to do instead of pressing you toward what you haven't yet resolved.

What matters going forward isn't whether you immediately seek out different rooms or reconfigure your calendar. What matters is that you no longer confuse familiarity with effectiveness. Once you understand how much influence a room has over how you think and operate, you start paying attention to signals you once ignored. You notice whether conversations demand clarity or allow ambiguity to linger. You notice whether expectations are explicit or assumed. You notice whether the environment still requires growth, or whether it's become a place where doing what you already know is enough. Whether responsibility and accountability are core tenets or platitudes.

This book ends here because the argument is complete. This book isn't about instruction, it's about awareness. From now on, every room you enter will teach you something, whether you intend it to or not. The only real choice is whether you notice what that lesson is and decide if it aligns with where you're trying to go.

Your decision doesn't *(necessarily)* need urgency. It needs honesty, and that's something no room can provide for you unless you're willing to see it first.

This is why I have included a special gift for you.

A Gift For You

I kept this book short because clarity doesn't come from volume. It comes from seeing the right patterns and knowing what to do with them.

The resources I'm offering here exist for one reason: to help you apply what you've just read in real situations, with real pressure, and real people involved. They aren't add-ons or bonuses. They're the working pieces behind the ideas in this book.

You can access them here:
www.MePlusUltra.com/Resources

Inside, you'll find access to three things.

1. The Business Bourbon & Cigars Workbook

This is the same working framework used inside our leadership rooms. It's designed to slow your thinking down, surface constraints, and force clarity around decisions that tend to stay unresolved. Leaders who take it seriously often see why certain issues keep circling without ever moving forward, and what needs to change for that to stop.

This isn't a recap of the book and it isn't motivational. It's a tool meant to be used, not admired.

2. Guest Spotlight Observation

This gives you the opportunity to observe a live Guest Spotlight session, one of the working sessions inside Me Plus Ultra.

Not to participate. To observe. You'll see how experienced operators present real issues, how those issues are pressure-tested in the room, and how quickly clarity forms when preparation and standards are non-negotiable. For many people, this is the moment they realize whether this kind of environment sharpens them or drains them.

3. Priority Consideration to Apply for the Business Bourbon & Cigars Leadership Retreat

You'll also receive priority consideration to apply for an upcoming Business Bourbon & Cigars leadership retreat.

This isn't a guarantee and it isn't a shortcut. It's recognition that reading this book and engaging with the work signals a mindset we take seriously. Applications remain selective, capacity is limited, and the standard doesn't change—but your interest won't be treated as casual.

None of this is required. None of it is designed to convince you.

It's here for leaders who recognize themselves in these pages and want to be deliberate about where they invest their time, attention, and relationships next. If that's you, you'll understand how to use what's been offered.

Epilogue

By now, you don't need another explanation of how rooms work. You've seen it in your own experience, whether you labeled it that way or not.

You already know which environments sharpen you and which ones simply accommodate you. You know where you're challenged to think more clearly, and where you're mostly affirmed for what you already do well. You know which relationships continue to show up when something real is on the line, and which ones fade the moment the context changes.

That awareness is the point this book was building toward.

What comes next isn't about chasing something new. It's about taking a hard look at where your time actually goes, who has access to your attention, and which relationships you continue to feed with energy and trust. Those investments are limited- whether you admit it or not- and they shape what you become long before the results show up.

The right rooms don't just influence decisions. They shape the people you do the next decade of work with. They create opportunities you couldn't have planned for, alliances that don't need to be negotiated, and relationships that hold when things get difficult. That doesn't happen by accident. It happens when capable people choose standards over convenience and keep choosing them over time.

At this point, the decision isn't abstract. You'll make it the next time you decide where to show up, who to sit with, and which conversations you take seriously. You don't need urgency to do that. You just need to stop pretending those choices don't matter.

That's where this book leaves you. Not with instructions, but with clarity and the responsibility that comes with it.

About the Author

While most people talk about building businesses, Scott Joseph has spent his life doing it and doing it well. He has built, owned, and scaled every company he's been involved with to a high level of success, staying accountable for outcomes through growth, reinvention, and changing market conditions. His perspective wasn't formed through theory or short-term wins, but through long-term ownership and decisions that continued to matter years after they were made.

Much of Scott's success has come from his ability to build teams and identify the right people early. He learned quickly that growth doesn't come from individual effort alone, but from assembling capable leaders, placing them in the right roles, and creating environments where they could operate without constant direction. Over time, that ability to judge people, build trust, and structure responsibility became a defining advantage across every business he touched.

As his companies grew, Scott began noticing something most leaders around him didn't. People with similar talent and work ethic were getting very different results, and it wasn't because of strategy or effort. It came down to who they were surrounded by and what those environments quietly demanded. That difference showed up over time in momentum, in decision quality, and in which relationships actually held when things got difficult.

Those observations, combined with a clear gap in the market, led to the creation of Me Plus Ultra, a private leadership consortium built for experienced operators who no longer need motivation, but do need rooms that challenge their thinking and expand what's possible through trusted relationships. The group has become a place where long-term partnerships form, referrals happen naturally, and strategic alliances emerge because members understand how one another actually operates.

Today, Scott's work centers on designing and participating in high-standard environments where leaders continue to sharpen their judgment, build meaningful relationships, and uncover new opportunities through proximity rather than promotion. His belief is simple and hard-earned: Sustained success is rarely limited by effort or intelligence, but by the quality of the rooms and the people leaders choose to grow alongside, and most leaders underestimate how much that choice is already shaping them.

Thank You

Thank you for spending your time with this book.

If anything in it made you pause or look at your own situation a little differently, that matters. Not because it proves a point, but because those moments tend to surface things we already sensed but hadn't named clearly yet.

What happens next doesn't need to be dramatic. The most meaningful changes usually come from paying closer attention to where you show up, who you stay connected to, and which conversations continue after the obvious ones end. Over time, those choices shape not just outcomes, but the quality of the work and the people you build alongside.

If this book helped sharpen how you see those choices, then it served its purpose. I appreciate you reading it and taking it seriously.
– Scott Joseph